Hits
and
Near Misses

a memoir

Ralph Sinsheimer

Copyright © 2025 by Ralph Sinsheimer

All rights reserved.

No part of this publication may be reproduced, distributed, or transmitted in any form or by any means, including photocopying, recording, or other electronic or mechanical methods, without the prior written permission of the publisher, except as permitted by U.S. copyright law.

For permission requests, contact Sinsheimer Literary by emailing max@sinsheimerliterary.com.

For privacy reasons, some names, locations, and dates may have been changed. Additionally, while this book is a work of non-fiction, some fictional elements may have seeped in for the sake of enhancing story continuity and to illuminate the characters and events.

Book cover and interior design by David Provolo.

ISBN (hardcover): 979-8-9991360-0-8
ISBN (eBook): 979-8-9991360-1-5

First Edition 2025

Back cover flap photo by Ellen Dubin Photography

For Amy

*Truly my better half, without whom this tale,
this life, would be sadness and dust*

Contents

PART ONE *15*

Chapter 1: Takajo *17*

Chapter 2: Ball of Confusion *31*

Chapter 3: Friendly Town – #9, #9 . . . . *39*

Chapter 4: Ancora Tu *63*

PART TWO *75*

Chapter 5: Swimming Upstream *77*

Chapter 6: Not Exactly Random *89*

Chapter 7: Craig Fuller:
              What you wanna do? *103*

Chapter 8: Going Downtown *125*

Chapter 9: Dirty Water *137*

Chapter 10: Looking Out the Window . . . *151*

Chapter 11: Eureka! Get Yer
             Red Hot Beer Here *161*

Chapter 12: The Glickenhaus Bridge *171*

PART THREE *187*

Chapter 13: From Partnership
             to Partnership *189*

Chapter 14: The Bad Seed *197*

Chapter 15: In Control. *203*

Chapter 16: Diagnosis *213*

Chapter 17: My Peeps *219*

Chapter 18: Planning for the Future *225*

Acknowledgements and Credits *237*

Preface

It is an article of faith that when writing one's memoir, the scope of the work should be tightly focused, the themes few, and the reader able to glean the author's positions. As a novice writer I can't say that I have acted on this very sensible advice. Instead, the book tends to go off the tracks in certain places, giving way to a tangent or a dangling antidote. I make no apologies for this since this is the way my cluttered mind seems to work.

I have taken on this writing project following my recent retirement in order to be productive and to stave off falling into a life of daytime TV soaps and mint chocolate chip ice cream. Beyond the need to DO SOMETHING, I have had a hankering to test my memory and to take on the challenge of expressing myself through a number of stories and impressions. I thank you, dear reader, for taking the time to read the following pages.

Although I have attempted to be as true to real events and people as possible, I have taken the liberty of salting in several fictional touches and found it necessary to change a few names. Additionally, I have refrained from identifying or discussing any of my investment and wealth advisory clients' business in deference to their privacy.

The primary audience I hope to reach with this book is my extraordinary family. My wife Amy, my mother and my late father, as well as my siblings, children, and grandchildren have been central characters in my life. I couldn't have asked for a better set of supporters, role models, teachers, playmates, etc.

My maternal and paternal family lines come down from Russia and Germany. My father's parents were born in New York City (Grandpa Jerry) and St. Louis (Grandma Betty). For some inexplicable reason her father moved Betty and the rest of the Berchansky family to the small town of Honey Grove, Texas, which was founded by Davy Crocket and located about eighty-five miles northeast of Dallas. According to my father, the Berchanskys were the only Jewish family in the community, and they owned and managed a general store overlooking the town square. Grandma Betty and family lived in the store's private second floor.

It may be that the move to Honey Grove was at least influenced by developments leading to the Galveston Plan. The idea of the Plan was to consider taking an intermediate step before reaching *the* Promised Land by first finding *a* promised land. The concept was Zionism without Zion and was led by the charismatic Theodorr Herzl and, later, by Israel Zangwill. Given the reality of the Ottoman Empire's long hold on Palestine, as well as the escalating atrocities befalling Jews around the world, there was a sense of urgency to find somewhere to create a Jewish state. In England, Chamberlain offered Herzl a portion of Britain's vast colonial holdings in East Africa to serve as a Jewish homeland. This would not be the only location that the

Annual Zionist Congress would debate and ultimately reject a magnanimous offer. However, when Galveston, Texas was put forth for consideration, it was green lit by a subgroup of Zionists who were part of the ITO (Jewish Territorial Organization). Although unlikely, my maternal great-grandfather may have been taken with Texas as a place to raise his family due to its open space and apparent openness to an influx of immigrant Jews.

Sinsheimer is a surname derived from the town of Sinsheim in southwestern Germany. Following the U.S. civil war, one prominent Sinsheimer family migrated from Sinsheim to San Luis Obispo, California, where they became very successful retail operators. Today, the town is filled with streets named Sinsheimer and evidence of their family's mercantilist prowess. I have no idea if our families are related. Or, for that matter, if we are related to the late Robert Sinsheimer, the award-winning Caltech quantitative biologist who became Chancellor of UC Santa Cruz. Whenever I asked Grandpa Jerry if this or that Sinsheimer was related to us he would always say yes to the ones who had sterling reputations and no to the ones who didn't measure up.

My maternal grandmother, Sylvia Rosenthal, married my namesake, Ralph Dubin, who died when my mother was only a teenager. Sylvia later married Henry Uttal, a lawyer who, seven years after their wedding, became incapacitated with progressive dementia. I remember being seated in our formal dining room in Scarsdale when we children were told that Henry had died. In the face of this sad news, I unaccountably began to laugh, and I couldn't stop doing so for a few minutes. Although quite young, I became concerned about whatever was inside me that caused this reaction. Sylvia would frequently visit us by train from New York City to our house in Scarsdale, so we called her Grandma

Choo-Choo. She was a real pistol who enjoyed a good laugh. If she heard that one of us was seeing someone new, she would unfailingly ask for the last name of our date in a ploy to ascertain if he or she was Jewish. Sylvia was a no-nonsense woman who deplored those who relied on taxis when walking was the better, healthier choice, and when inexpensive, reliable public buses were readily available.

Grandma Choo-Choo's aunt, Anne Phillips (née Rosenthal), had three children, including Libby Phillips, who married Bernie Marcus. Bernie's father, Joseph, was a shirtmaker who kept a safe at his Lower East Side place of business. Because his neighbors were, like him, immigrants—most of whom did not speak English—they preferred to keep their money in Joseph's safe. Before long, Joseph became a banker, and in mid-1913 he founded what became the third-largest bank in New York and one of the top thirty largest banks in the country, The Bank of the United States. Bernie took over from his father in 1919, and by 1930 the bank had close to five hundred thousand depositors and sixty-two branches, up from five locations a decade earlier, and had taken on a very high level of commercial real estate debt. The bank's appellation gave the false impression that it was backed by the federal government, especially to its immigrant depositors. In mid-December 1930, it became the largest commercial bank failure in U.S. history. The Bank of the United States was sound but susceptible to a rumor-induced run. The Federal Reserve of New York drafted a plan to save the bank, but the Clearing House banks, led by J.P. Morgan, refused to implement it. Some believe that by not stabilizing the bank when they could have, the Clearing House banks inadvertently deepened the catastrophic depression that followed, culminating in the Bank Holiday of March 1933. The economist Milton Friedman and others laid much of the blame on antisemitism, particularly that of John Pierpont Morgan, Jr., who became embittered by the Jewish lawyers and businessmen that had subjected his father to public humiliation during the 1913 "Money Trust" congressional investigations. Among those who Morgan reserved for his vituperative rage was Louis Brandeis and Samual Untermyer, the latter acted as counsel to the congressional committee investigating the House of Morgan and other large banks. J.P. Morgan, Jr. had found a way to get even—but at what cost?

Bernie Marcus was also culpable. His appetite for acquisitions and the dizzying number of subsidiaries he created led to fraudulent bookkeeping, for which he served prison time.

As a footnote, Bernie was a favorite uncle of Roy Cohn, the notorious, repulsive aide to Senator Joseph McCarthy and mentor to Donald Trump. Bernie and Libby were close to Cohn, and Roy would often visit Bernie at Sing Sing, where he served out his prison term. I am told that my familial linkage to the shifty-eyed Cohn is sufficiently weak that it relieves me of any concerns I might have about sharing Cohn's evil blood.

Both of my parents had one sibling, Seth Dubin in my mother's case, and Michelle Feins, known as Mickey, in my father's. I adored Mickey as I do Seth. Aunt Mickey was refreshingly kooky. She went through a few phases, including becoming a

Jew for Jesus. She was seven years younger than my dad, and as the two of them got older, their tight bond strengthened further. Uncle Seth has always been intellectually inquisitive and interested in ideas, politics, and people. Not only does he make an effort to keep in touch with his nephews and nieces, but he has also remained an important figure in my son Max's life. The two of them have books, England, and Oxford University Press in common.

I have always appreciated how lucky I am to have such wonderful parents, siblings and their spouses. We enjoy and respect each other immensely. My mother instilled in me a love for books, the arts in general, and a keen interest in understanding what makes people who they are. She also taught me to look first to the redeeming qualities of a person before jettisoning them from consideration in my life. I recall coming upstairs to my parents' bedroom at the end of a night out and, with my dad fast asleep—weary from transatlantic travel and the cruelty of time zone changes—mom would put her book down and ask me to tell her all about my evening. My sister Linda is the one who best absorbed mom's fascination and facility with people. Linda never ceases to amaze me with her thirst for social exchanges and the loving, often time-consuming support she gives her kids and grandkids.

Before his death at the end of January 2024, my father imparted to us adult children the importance of living a principled, ethical life and striving for achievement. He believed that a good education is a primary contributor to the enrichment and, ultimately, advancement in one's life. That is probably why he and my mother created an endowed scholarship at NYU Law School administered under the Ruth Tilden umbrella. For selected students, the fellowship pays 100% of the total cost of school. In return, Sinsheimer Fellows commit to spending three years in public service after graduation. My father also created a not-for-profit law firm, Legal Services for Children (later renamed Partnership for Children's Rights and ultimately merged into the Mobilization for Justice) which fights for the rights of disabled, disadvantaged kids in New York City who have not been given the specialized educational support they are entitled to by law. His sharp legal mind—as well as his tinkering, engineer's brain—found its way into my brother Alan's methodical and mathematically inclined mind. Michael, the youngest of my parents' children, exhibits the sweetness and thoughtfulness of my mother and the tenacious, goal-driven business focus of my father.

Linda's husband, Rob Moser, was the first in-law of my generation, and he set the bar high. Rob is a patient, even keeled, and caring man who is a pleasure to be around. Lisa, Alan's wife, is an intriguing woman, and I admit that in the very early days of her relationship with Alan, I was a bit wary of her. She seemed too anxious to impress, too ready to raise her voice above others so she would be the one heard. But I had misjudged Lisa and as she began to feel more confident in her acceptance into the Sinsheimer clan, she softened and became the truly wonderful sister-in-law that she is. Whip-smart, empathetic, and always interesting, Lisa does Alan great credit. Michael's wife, Anne, has been a terrific partner for my brother. She has physical and behavioral traits that are similar to Amy, my wife, whom you'll read more about in the pages ahead. As for Anne, we only wish we could bridge the distance between her homes in the Carolinas and ours in New York.

Part One

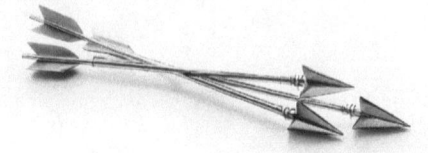

Chapter 1

Takajo

It is a cool, blustery Saturday in early November, and the leaves quicken their frantic aerial dance. Even some of the most colorful have fallen and turned gunmetal gray. Autumn and spring are my favorite seasons, but the post-summer period is bittersweet, with its fragile beauty and its call inward to self-reflect. Outside, the incessant whine of leaf blowers carries through my bedroom window from several nearby yards. Surely there will be no need for the gardeners to return in the coming weeks.

Fall 1963, and America is transfixed by a culturally sophisticated and engaged White House, a mushrooming Cold War, and a space race whose key players keep leapfrogging one another's technological advancements. Stirrings of discontent with America's burgeoning role in the Southeast Asian conflict are creeping into the consciousness of the nation, and a powerful civil rights movement is brewing.

I am a month shy of my ninth birthday, which will be marred by the assassination of President John F. Kennedy. At

11 a.m. on November 25th, three days after JFK's death, Mr. Albanese, the janitor at my elementary school, wheeled a clunky RCA black-and-white TV set into the classroom and plugged it in. Miss Spiegelman, our third-grade teacher, explained that we can watch the late president's funeral. She switched on the TV and tuned in to Channel 2, the New York CBS affiliate station and home to news anchor Walter Cronkite, who had three days earlier barely held in check his quavering voice as he reported JFK's passing. The impact the broadcast made on us was indelible. From the veiled beauty of the president's mourning wife, Jackie, to the bathos of her three-year-old son's iconic salute during his father's funeral procession, we never forgot the cleaving of our world into a *before* and an *after*. I would come to understand that these tragic inflection points are not as rare as I believed when I was young.

Despite their youth, the assassination and the end of Camelot accelerated the maturation of a few of my classmates, who began to consider how their education and activism could help them make a difference in the world. But most of us were pre-political and held on to our little world just a bit longer.

In 1963, the Beatles and the British Invasion are still a year away. On the radio, the number one song is the Ronettes' "Be My Baby." The song is everywhere, on every transistor radio. Peripatetic. It was produced by Phil Spector, whose "wall-of-sound" production techniques would influence countless producers including the deeply talented yet extremely disturbed Brian Wilson of the Beach Boys. Brian's "I Can Hear Music" is just one of the many songs on which Brian employed a powerful wall of triple-looped vocal harmonies. Spector also had many detractors stemming from his excessive, bombastic style of production. Paul McCartney was so upset with Spector's addition of soaring, self-important strings on his song "Long and Winding Road", that he remixed and reissued it without keeping the string tracks.

A very different sensibility can be heard elsewhere on the radio dial. That summer's chart-topping hit is about homesickness from summer camp, titled "Hello Muddah, Hello Fadduh" by Allen Sherman. It's a novelty song, strictly for laughs, but it has me, a prospective first-time camper, a little bit on edge.

About two miles away, Morty Goldman exits the Hutchinson Parkway, steadily closing in on our house. Morty is still ruggedly handsome at 48. His alert blue eyes twinkle kindness. His face is creased and deeply tanned from his daily summer exertions on the tennis courts, soccer fields, and in the boats docked by the floating waterfront on pristine Long Lake. He built Camp Takajo in 1947, and every year thereafter he has made off-season camper recruitment trips to those northeastern towns with a concentration of well-off, assimilated Jews. His meetings cluster in the well-tended suburbs of Philadelphia's Main Line, Boston's Brookline and Newton, Long Island's Five Towns, and Westchester's Scarsdale and Rye.

Morty steers his nearly new Chevrolet Corvette C2 Stingray off the Hutchinson Parkway toward Murray Hill Road in Scarsdale, New York. He is not given to flashy acquisitions, but he has an eye for beauty, and the Stingray's sleek, futuristic design thrills him. The exhilaration of driving this head-turner of an automobile, as well as his embrace of the Takajo mission, impels him on his appointed rounds.

Morty pulls his Corvette into the driveway, gathers his Takajo tote bag containing his carousel of slides, and parks in front of the gracious white Colonial. He notes the recently swept Har-Tru tennis court in the backyard. All of us in the family play tennis with varying degrees of competence and interest. The exception is my middle brother, Alan, fourteen months my junior, who eschews most sports but will become a member of Choate and Princeton's ultimate frisbee teams. He'll also race sailboats on Long Island Sound and become coxswain on one of Princeton's rowing shells.

Morty finishes his surveillance of the Sinsheimer yard, and just as he reaches for the doorbell, the door swings open. "Ah, you must be Ralph," he says.

That afternoon, the picture Morty paints for me and my parents is nirvana. Had I any concerns about leaving my "Muddah and Faddah" for seven summer weeks, they are totally dashed. Over his hour-plus visit, Morty dwells equally on the importance of Takajo's six pillars—Integrity, Tolerance, Sportsmanship, Friendliness, Self-Reliance, and Magnanimity—as well as the physical beauty of the campus and the vast array of activities available to campers. He brings out his Kodak carousel of slides depicting the multitude and quality of bunks, athletic facilities, the lodge, dining hall, waterski dock, archery and rifle shooting galleries, art center, Indian council ring of fire, theater playhouse, nature building, and adjacent animal pens.

I can barely contain myself as I imagine becoming a popular camper whose athletic prowess is admired throughout camp. In my mind's eye I can see myself as a seven-year Takajo camper, which would mean I'd receive the special "T" sweater and be considered for inclusion on the Senior Western trip, an invitation that anoints the recipient as one who has achieved a high level of physical, intellectual, and emotional maturation. My excitement reaches its apotheosis in mid-June, on the eve of my first bus ride north to Naples, Maine, where Camp Takajo is perched on the southern shore of the 2-by-9-mile Long Lake.

Two gleaming chartered buses—both refitted green-and-white Peter Pans—board their passengers at a rendezvous spot in the parking lot of the Crowne Plaza in White Plains. Every seat is taken by Takajo campers, counselors, and staff. The seemingly endless six-hour ride is made bearable by the learning and singing of camp songs, from the heartfelt "We Will Ere Remember" to more rousing tunes such as "99 Bottles of Beer on the Wall" and "Come 'Round Any Old Time."

The long bus ride up to Naples also offers us the opportunity to begin connecting with our peers. I sit next to Ricky Sokolov, a warm-hearted extrovert with an inviting smile and an appreciation for good humor, be it the ice-cream-on-a-stick kind or the funny kind. He is very easy to talk to, and we became good friends. Across the aisle sits Richie Finn, a soft spoken, modest boy with a pouty expression, who turns out to be a dominant tennis player and among the best all-around athletes in the camp's youngest (Warrior) section.

Also on the bus is my good friend from home, Biff Blashek. We would become lifelong best friends, but our long-term friendship was not assured at this point. As much as we enjoyed each other's company (and we really did), we didn't always agree on things and at times we had varying recollections of shared events. Both of us could be quite stubborn. I believed that I had already adopted Takajo's tenets and was an exemplar of tolerance and magnanimity. But in fact, I was no angel and during junior high school, I began to pick up friendship demerits by the handful. The biggest was an outgrowth of a fight over events that, of course, I can no longer recall. Still, as far as I was concerned, we were no longer friends.

A few years later, during the one summer Biff didn't attend Takajo, I badmouthed him to our mutual friends. He would learn of my hurtful betrayal and call me out on it. Notwithstanding my petty barbs uttered at a time when his absence meant that he could not defend himself, Biff still included me in his Bar Mitzvah celebration. I, on the other hand, did not invite him to my birthday party, which was celebrated by bringing six of my friends to a Doors concert. The concert was held in Assembly Hall at Hunter College on November 24, 1967, my actual 13th birthday. The Doors released their eponymous first album in January of that year and its follow-up, *Strange Days*, had just recently arrived in record stores. Seeing the leather-clad Jim Morrison with a small group of my friends burnished my cool quotient, which I had no intention of allowing Biff to dilute.

Our bus finally pulls into the camp's private, half mile-long dirt road, swings right at the welcome arch that displays the six pillars, and parks by a cluster of tennis courts. We all cheer, file out, and mill around as we await the return of our duffel bags from the belly of the bus. I look around. The scale of the property is impressive, and I take a deep breath. Inhale, exhale. And again: inhale, exhale. By the second breath I notice the pleasantly intoxicating scent of fir trees and pine sap, which I associate with Christmas.

Yes, we were those kinds of Jews who quietly celebrated Christmas, much to the disapproval of my grandmother. We would crowd the tree with hanging ornaments and silvery tinsel. The tree, for the week leading up to December 25, was tantalizing, surrounded by presents galore. Mom and Dad went all in, but I believe they managed to keep from crossing the line into the realm of child spoilers. As for our own heritage, we would light the menorah candles during the first few nights of Hanukkah, but lack of interest curtailed this practice for the last four or five nights of the holiday. We had no regular Friday night Shabbat routine, nor would I ever feel comfortable trying to lip sync the Hebrew blessing over the bread.

I remember that first afternoon at Takajo with a vivid clarity. Counselors manned tables at several nearby drop-off points. These nondescript stations bore clearly marked signs indicating the correct age tier they were set up to welcome: Warrior, Junior, or Senior. At the tables, campers received their bunk assignments and day-one schedules. I waited in line until I came face to face with one of the counselors seated at the table. His name was Arnie Abrams, a husky collegiate with a riot of curly blonde hair and a face pitted with acne. He asked for my name, age, and hometown. I responded, and he checked my name off his list and gave me a small packet with a camp map, a sign-up sheet for several clubs, a flyer from the music director soliciting interest in being cast in the summer musical—the Lionel Bart hit show *Oliver!*—and a notice that within the next few days, all new campers would need to take a swim test. I was to spend my first Takajo summer in bunk Winnebago along with seven other boys and two counselors.

During that initial summer in Maine, I was exposed to, and embraced, the quirky traditions and lore of Takajo. I will never know why I agreed to join the Dippy Club, which required its members to jump out of bed at the trumpeter's first notes of reveille each morning at 6:30, grab a towel, run down to the waterfront, and dive into the often ridiculously cold Long Lake. The sunrise was not yet old enough to provide any warmth, and I was not the only dippy to turn blue on the run back to our bunks.

Each camper class had its own head overseer and all three invariably stamped their own imprimatur on the summer experience of their campers and the counselors who reported to him. Artie Benickson was the head overseer of the Warriors. Art's facial features were possum-like. He was short and bald, save patches of hair on both sides of his head, just above his ears. His thin nose curved slightly upward to a narrow point, and his obsidian eyes were beady.

Notwithstanding his unattractive mien, Artie was one of the camp's favorite figures. He enjoyed singling out campers who had achieved something meaningful and rewarding them in public with one of his purple turtles, of which he seemed to have an endless supply. The conferring of these small plastic creatures thrilled the recipients, and most placed a very high value on the prize, as if the turtles were made of gold.

Once a week, Artie would don a full Native American outfit complete with an authentic headdress that featured a long feather trailer, and a breastplate made of buffalo bones decorated with intricate beadwork. From his seat at the Indian Council Ring of Fire, Artie would call out to the entire camp by pounding on an oversized, deeply resonant Tom-Tom drum. DUM dum dum dum… DUM dum dum dum… DUM dum dum dum. Once all the campers had filed into the council ring and were seated, Artie would hand the drum mallets to another counselor, who would continue beating them while Artie danced in his tasseled leather moccasins around the bonfire burning brightly in the middle of the ring. He would then be given a long, feathered pipe from which he filled his mouth and blew a steady stream of smoke while pointing the pipe to each of the four corners of the world. He then bellowed out a Native American prayer to Mother Nature and invited anyone else to give their thanks for the beauty and bounty that sustained us all. Although some of the older campers rolled their eyes, we Warriors ate it up.

Artie was just one of the many characters who worked at Takajo. Joe "Bat" Batatelle headed the Intermediate camp group. An Italian American, he had a mild stutter and when he felt it coming on, he would clutch his ever-present clipboard tighter. The Senior camp head, Milt Greenberg, always seemed to be holding back an explosive tirade or gleeful celebration. His raspy voice registered within a very narrow range, and it was only by careful observation that you might glimpse a pulsing vein at the side of his neck. This signaled anger and meant you should avoid confronting him at all costs.

Our daily routine generally included playing at least one sport in the morning and one in the afternoon. Likewise, you were expected to participate in other non-sports activities such as art, nature, and theater in the morning and/or the afternoon.

There was free time for other activities like sailing, waterskiing, and so on. I most enjoyed participating in soccer and baseball, and waterskiing. After dinner, we played cards, talked about girls and our baseball heroes, washed up, and got into our beds. Lights out times varied but once set were strictly enforced. If a counselor on Quad duty heard chatter from the bunk, he would silently sneak up and, from one of the unobscured screened windows, point a powerful flashlight into the bunk and spotlight the culprit. At that point the guilty boy, now temporarily blinded, might be told to go outside and hug a tree for an undetermined period. Or, if the counselor had just come back from cocktails with his female counterpart at Mattaponi, our nearby sister camp, he might simply sing to you. Our Junior bunk counselor, Richie Fire, would often belt out the Rolling Stones' lyrics "Don't play with me 'cause you're playing with fire." He was so cool.

Over the course of my Takajo summers, I participated in a few camping trips. I learned the basics of camping, which called for clear-eyed planning. For the more strenuous mountain hikes—particularly those that were overnighters—this meant guarding against altitude sickness by beginning a regimen of twice-daily chlorophyll gels several days in advance of the hike. I learned not only what to pack, but also how to optimally arrange our backpacks to fit and access key items. These included safety devices such as red flares and bear spray, and adequate layers of clothing to brace us against the drop in temperatures to be expected at altitudes exceeding 6,000 feet.

Food and water needed to be handled carefully and judiciously meted out to ensure they would not be fully depleted before our descent down the mountain was completed. On two occasions I was part of a group of three to five campers deemed capable and fit enough to scale Mt. Katahdin and Mt. Washington, the two highest peaks in New England. For the Katahdin hike we were escorted by John Jordan and for Mt. Washington, we were led by Roger Goldman, a serious mountain climber and the older son of Morty, the camp's founder and owner.

After our ascent of Katahdin, I was not keen to participate in the forthcoming climb up Mt. Washington. I had a difficult time during the last quarter of the Katahdin hike and had some doubts about my ability and the durability of my luck for this next and highest peak. It was a moderate crisis of confidence. Nerves or not, I would rise to the challenge.

I took on the Mt. Washington climb not because I was a natural competitor, but rather because I so admired Roger and the entire Goldman clan, a family with a larger-than-life, fairy tale quality to them. Morty, his regal wife Elise—whose blizzard of black and gray hair sat in a loose beehive swirl—and their four grown children. Roger was the oldest, Judy was the cool, cerebral activist, John was the camp's reveille and taps bugler, and the very attractive Nancy was a budding thespian whose participation as the leading lady in the summer play was the reason so many campers tried out to be her leading man. The Goldmans were endowed with striking beauty, robust intellect, social fluency and a commitment to helping those who were in need. Somehow, they seemed to be utterly unaffected by their good fortune. They shared a certain intense social liberalism.

In addition to the prospect of spending time with Roger

and getting to know him on the trail and by the campfire (at least as much as any 13-year-old can get to know someone in his early 20s). I was keen to learn more about the post-camp Western Senior trip, which I would be eligible for during my final season at Takajo. What transpired during this annual two-week trip was kept secret. Although in earlier years many of the counselors had participated in the Senior trip as their last camp hurrah, not one of them would discuss details of their trip, which inflamed both my interest and my curiosity.

The physical difficulty I encountered during the ascent of Mt. Washington was compounded by my growing sense that Roger was a private man, not naturally loquacious. But it turned out that I was wrong. Once we made camp for the night and the strain of the hike was behind us, we had a great discussion about music, politics, and relationships. And while I recognized that Roger was simply being the sweet guy that he was, I felt singled out. We talked about his friendship with John Wideman, a new counselor who was a classmate of Roger's sister, Judy, at Penn. John was very impressive, imposing. He was born and raised in a very tough area of Pittsburgh known as Homewood. A top student, he was given a full scholarship to attend the University of Pennsylvania. John was only the second black man to become a Rhodes Scholar, and he was by far the best basketball player I had ever seen up close. An absolute phenom. In 1963, Gene Shalit wrote a piece in *Look* magazine titled "The Amazing John Wideman." The fawning would continue.

What I didn't know before my campfire talk with Roger was that John and Judy were a very serious couple and had just—very quietly—announced their engagement to Judy's family. At that time, I don't think I could point to many mixed-race couples, but Morty's enthusiastic blessing of John and Judy's union was what I would expect from a paragon of enlightened liberalism.

In later years, I would follow John's public milestones with great interest. His career as an author and teacher was a spectacular success. He was the only author to win the prestigious Pen/Faulkner award twice. He was selected as a Macarthur Fellow and a finalist for the National Book Award and the National Book Critics Circle Award. John became one of the leading intellectuals in the country, and a much sought-after teacher, with stints at the University of Wyoming, University of Pennsylvania, Amherst College in Massachusetts, and Brown University.

But away from the lights and the heady awards, nothing would prove as easy as a layup for the talented Wideman.

Chapter 2

Ball of Confusion

Takajo was not just a meaningful and fun place to be, it was also a refuge from the increasingly complex world I faced in Scarsdale. I was not a model student and was tested for dyslexia. Although I never met them, I got to know the Billings family, whose telephone number was the same as mine, other than the inversion of the last two digits. After my first several misdialed calls to her household, Mrs. Billings recognized my voice and gently reminded me that I needed to redial my house using the correct number.

My parents were friends with Betty and Al Osman, and I was a friend of their son, Dick Osman. Betty was a child psychologist with a specialty in learning disabilities—she literally wrote the book on the subject. For at least a year, I had hour-long sessions with her twice a week. Moreover, much to my embarrassment, Dick, a model student, was engaged to tutor me in math and science. It was one thing to lay bare my learning issues to his mom, who was a generation removed from me, and quite another to struggle through sessions with a peer. I sometimes felt as if I were wearing a neon placard with the word "idiot" blinking brightly.

From grade school to the middle of junior high, I was quite happy and socially adept. I made and maintained friendships effortlessly, and my social circle was as diverse as could be had in a homogenous community like Scarsdale. I was a bit too proud of my father's success in business, which enabled him and my mother to raise us in a comfortable setting without physical or monetary fears. Their love was given to me and my siblings unconditionally.

My parents led busy lives and traveled frequently. In the press, my father was dubbed the David Frost of the business world—a reference to the media star interviewer who crisscrossed the Atlantic many times each year.

Often on weekends and unscheduled after-school afternoons, our yard would be the site of an organized pick-up game or just a few guys passing a football or soccer ball around. My group included some very smart and, ultimately, very successful boys. These included Tom Rogers, who ran NBC cable and TiVo; future architect Jeff Fein; intellectual and acclaimed academic David Scobey; and cello-playing Evan Beenhower. There was also Jimmy Handelman, whose terrible eyesight required extremely thick glasses and who favored wearing cowboy outfits every day, even after he became the Executive Director of a large foundation. Another early friend was Michael Epstein, a boy-wonder businessman who in the fourth grade founded the Norma Tanega ("Walking My Cat Named Dog") fan club, which cost me $4 to join. By his second year out of college, Michael was also the genius behind multiple, extremely profitable luxury car dealerships, as well as other business schemes. Michael, who was early to declare his homosexuality, seemed quite happy with his husband, Scott, and life in Beverly Hills. Sadly, decades later he committed suicide for reasons I will never know.

Others included all-around nice guy Doug Hobe, long-haired Robby Spain, and Rob Blashek, who dropped the nickname "Biff" in favor of his real name just before he matriculated at Brown University. Rob had a streak of outrage for the irresponsible and entitled. He was keenly aware of a societal pecking order, and while he never begrudged families their wealth, he did rail against those in the next generation who were spoiled and seemingly allergic to work and responsibility. He also was extremely loyal, a trait I leaned into when I became persona non grata in several homes.

I had my first taste of Martha's Vineyard when Robby Spain's family hosted me at their up-island home overlooking Menemsha harbor. To say that it was an idyllic week is to do the island a disservice. Robby never wore shoes, and he and I smoked cigarettes despite our youth. Robby's older brother looked a lot like Bob Dylan and even wore the same corduroy newsboy cap that Dylan donned on the cover of his eponymous first album. I vaguely recall that he was smitten with a neighborhood beauty named Elizabeth Klufner, who was known as EK. She was tall, ginger-haired, and had a dancer's posture that accentuated her exceptional figure. In fact, she entered Juilliard with the hope of becoming a professional dancer. I would spend many summers and sporadic fall and spring weekends on the Vineyard once my parents decided to rent and then buy a house on the island. For several decades, the Vineyard was a touchstone place for me.

I had many friends, but beginning in seventh grade I made poor choices regarding how I divided my time between my old group, who were generally motivated to succeed in school, and the so-called cool crowd who were... less so. Curiously, many of these newer friends had gone to Edgewood or Greenacres Elementary schools. They included Whitey Whickham, David Yarborough, Peter Schneider, and Greg Kirkpatrick.

I found them to be daring and unafraid. We would sometimes hop trains to White Plains station from the Scarsdale village by jumping onto the back of the last train car just as it was leaving the station. Once in White Plains, we would just hang, walk the streets, or shoplift a record or two from Macy's. After a few successful attempts, I became convinced that I was invisible, and that if I appeared to already own the LPs, no one would suspect me of stealing.

One time I was at the store with Peter Schneider, a terrific guy but not quite as gutsy as the others. Peter was short, with a button nose reminiscent of Paddington Bear and ears that stuck out, which gave him a mousy appearance. While I circled the record department racks, Peter kept a safe distance. I took a pile of LPs—as many as 11 or 12—and walked out the door unscathed. Peter, who had not taken anything, was delighted with my "haul," and after a few blocks asked if he could have one or two of my newly purloined records. Just as he grabbed Moby Grapes's eponymous debut album from my pile, he was tapped on the shoulder by the Macy's security guard, who said to us both, "Come with me, NOW."

We were taken to a drab, poorly lit basement office where the guard and a colleague questioned us while we sat on cold metal chairs. "What does your father do for a living?" he asked me. "He's a lawyer," I answered. "Well, do you want to see how good he is?" he bellowed back to me. His colleague turned to Peter. "And what about you, what does your father do?" Peter was so scared that he burst out crying, sobbing "my father's dead and my mother can't support us. I was born with a hole in my heart, and it feels like it's going to explode right now." Where the hell did that come from, I thought. I could have kissed him. In the span of 30 seconds Peter had managed to turn our interrogators from noir film tough guys to romcom softies. They let us go and neither of us ever returned to that Macy's or stole another record from anywhere again.

And then there was David Karp, nicknamed Dud, a truncated version of Duddy. He was naturally street smart and had one of the sharpest wits I had ever encountered. He could really make you cry laughing, but his was the kind of humor that came at the expense of others. Although he rarely sang for us, he had a remarkably moving voice, particularly when he sang "When a Man Loves a Woman," sounding note for note as good as, if not better than Percy Sledge.

David and his older brother Howie hosted a regular poker game in which the stakes were way too high for normal kids our age. His mother and father seemed to have checked out of parenting, and they were often traveling or unavailable. There didn't seem to be any boundaries set. Dud was an early user, and in a few years, when he began to slur his words and lose acuity, I suspected that he was sinking deeper into drugs. For several years I generally kept my distance from David and watched while his addiction took hold. There were several of us who confronted him, but to no avail. I had lost one high school friend to drugs (Bruce Black), and it amazed me that David survived for as long as he did. He succumbed to his habit in his 40s.

My own drug use was limited to occasional pot and hashish smoking. For much of ninth grade, I would join one or more of my friends at "Piss Rock," which was situated within the woods that abutted the high school grounds. There, we would smoke cigarettes and pass a joint around. I was careful to avoid getting too high, and I rarely had my own marijuana or hash to offer. I was very paranoid about losing control and being found out. The first—and nearly last—time I took psilocybin, I hallucinated a policeman.

Paranoid or not, I still flirted with incredibly risky, totally stupid behavior. One evening during ninth grade I attended the Spider's Web, an annual school dance. I brought with me a bottle of Seconal pills that I had pilfered from my parents' medicine chest. Dolly Durham, believed to be a "fast" girl, asked me to give her some pills for her and her friend Gene. However, Dolly decided not to share her pills with Gene. The resultant overdose required her stomach to be pumped and had the police searching for the person who provided Dolly with the pills. This was on the eve of winter vacation, and I was due to travel with my family to Jamaica the next day. How lucky, I thought. How fortuitous. By the time I return home, the entire nightmare will be forgotten. But certainly not by me.

Surrounded by turquoise and coral beauty for eleven days, all I could imagine were even more tragic outcomes for Dolly, which would weigh on my conscience for many years to come. In the week and a half that I was in the Caribbean, the Scarsdale police had not been idle, and the local papers carried the story. As soon as we returned, my parents put together the fact of Dad's missing sleeping pills, my inability to smile on vacation, and the terrible reports of the Spider's Web that appeared in the *Scarsdale Inquirer*. Over and over, I denied my involvement but finally told them the truth.

As expected, my parents were irate. Worse than that, they were disappointed. My father called the Scarsdale Police Department and explained that I was the guilty perpetrator who imperiled my classmate, leading the authorities to shut down the Spider's Web dance. The police responded that the call from my father was appreciated and came just as they were going to pay us an unannounced visit. I was remanded to my father's custody and he, in turn, brought me to a local judge and asked him what an appropriate punishment would be. I never found out exactly how he responded and wasn't keen to. Something about a parole period. This episode was a wake-up call for me, and I would reflect on it often—especially the fact that I lied to my parents and held on to that lie for so long. They had always been loving, fair, and generous. What was wrong with me?

Chapter 3

Friendly Town – #9, #9

The Spider's Web dance affair led my parents to strongly recommend to me that I go away to prep school. And since I had barely attended classes during my first year of high school, it was determined that I would redo my freshman year. Although I don't think I had a real choice, I agreed with them. We visited several schools, mostly in Connecticut and Massachusetts. I favored Mt. Hermon, which we toured on a gorgeous spring day.

The quad was filled with students, many with long hair, all clearly enjoying themselves. They were dressed in well-worn bell bottoms and Frye boots, strumming guitars, playing cards, or tossing frisbees. Several couples holding hands dotted the gently sloping rise leading out of the quad. This felt like my place. My parents noted this and determined that a loose, liberal environment was exactly what I did *not* need. Instead, I would attend the (initially) all-male, more conservative Wilbraham Academy starting in the early fall of 1969. This would change the trajectory of my life.

HITS AND NEAR MISSES

The summer leading up to my matriculation at Wilbraham was eventful. The Woodstock festival snarled traffic and announced to the country that youth culture had been super-sized. It was the summer of Apollo 11 and Neil Armstrong's breakthrough moon walk. Tragically, the summer of 1969 also witnessed the extreme violence of cult leader Charles Manson, who murdered the beautiful actress Sharon Tate and four others. And it was to be my last summer at Camp Takajo. I had outgrown the structured confines of the camp and although I would miss the opportunity to participate in the Western trip, I wanted to spend my last summer at home with my family and old circle of friends before taking the three-plus-hour drive to Wilbraham Academy—my new home away from home.

I was a little early to school and, not knowing anyone, I decided to stroll alone for a short distance on Main Street into the small town of Wilbraham. The town was configured in a six-by-eight-block grid. In the center stood a well-kept Friendly's eatery, which I would come to frequent. Besides its hamburgers, Friendly's was revered for its ice cream. The chain had hundreds of restaurants spread out across the Northeast. Wilbraham happened to be the site of Friendly's headquarters, which, in my eyes, put the town on the map. I had a particular love of their Fribbles, milkshakes so thick that straws effortlessly stood up straight in the serving glass. It required strong lungs to suck in its delicious contents.

After 30 minutes, I ambled back to the Academy. Like nearly 85% of the boarding students, my dorm was in the imposing Rich Hall, a massive brick building first built in 1804, the year the Academy was established. Rich Hall was multipurposed. Besides its dorm rooms on four of its floors, the first floor of Rich Hall housed the primary administrative offices, various deans' offices (including the Dean of Students and the Dean of Finance), the switchboard, and the cafeteria which stepped down to the unkempt basement-level student lounge. The entrance opened into a very large, dark cherry wood-paneled room whose ceilings accommodated the double-tall front doors. Several portraits of previous headmasters hung from the walls. An antique grandfather clock chimed on the hour. This entranceway served as a meeting place as well as an unsigned crossroads. The oversized room was a hive of activity as students entered and exited the building, coming and going to classes, activities, or meals.

Most classes were taught in buildings on the hill across from Main Street and Rich Hall. With some exceptions, each of these housed classrooms clustered by subject matter. Walking to the top of the hill, there was a path leading into the woods. About ¾ of a mile up the path, the woods opened to a small reservoir. This was the site of soulful reflection, especially for those of us who eschewed the Academy's chapel. The "Rez" was also a place to drink and smoke cigarettes or pot.

My dorm room was located on the penultimate, fourth floor of Rich Hall. My roommate was Chris Rausch, who lived in nearby Springfield. Chris could have been enrolled as a day student, but instead he and his parents opted for the more immersive option of living on campus. Day students numbered about 200—or nearly half of the student body—and at least in the early going, they tended to keep to themselves. Chris was painfully shy and terribly boring. He took a while to warm up. We would never be close friends, but over time I found his funny bone and we got along fine.

I became fast friends with several of my classmates, and a few sophomores and juniors. These included James Downey, David Shenk, Tim Platt, Jon Davis, and sophomore Charlie Woods from the Baltimore area.

David came from Lancaster, PA, and was the adopted child of older parents. His mother taught literature at the nearby Millersville University of Pennsylvania. His father was the first non-Steinman family member to be named Chairman of the largest media company in the region. He led Lancaster Newspapers and other enterprises owned by the Steinmans including Delmarva Broadcasting Company.. Their gracious house was in an idyllic part of the county, filled with undulating hills and vast farmlands on which tall, weathered grain silos and well-fed cows could be seen in great numbers.

David's hometown friends were unexceptional thrill seekers in a Bruce Springsteen way. They knew their cars and had no compunction about driving them fast. In the farmyards and well-paved roads outside Lancaster, it was not unusual to see cars that had been souped up or enhanced by replacing, say, original factory-installed stick shifts with top-of-the-line pistol grip shift handles from Hurst Billet.

David was not much of a student, and he wasn't much of a romantic. He was bold and seemed indifferent about making a fool of himself. David ran up to me one afternoon to ask whether I would join him and his friend Bob Jenkins and three nursing students he had met. David had "rustled up some ladies," and he planned an evening rendezvous for all six of us. Invariably, there would be no sizzle and very little steak. The girls were neither outgoing nor attractive. I felt awkward in these forced circumstances and would have to navigate them as they became more frequent.

Jon Davis was raised in New York City and upstate New York. The furthest thing from a city kid, he much preferred staying on Milfer Farm, the 1,000+-acre farm his family owned in Unadilla, just southwest of Oneonta, NY. Jon valued his privacy and initially appeared standoffish and cool. He was moody and leery of people. He was not very articulate and therefore not much of a communicator. Still, once he befriended and came to trust you, he would do anything for you. His difficulty expressing himself did not diminish the quality of his thinking or the depth of his feelings. He was extremely loyal and expected the same from others. He had a great capacity for work beyond what was expected of him, particularly when he found himself up against something that he couldn't break through in the normal allotted time. He applied more than once to Cornell's College of Veterinary Medicine before being accepted. Jon and I became roommates in our sophomore year and remained so through our senior year.

Jon's parents made for an odd couple. His mother was New York society—a demure opera enthusiast with perfect, lilting diction. Jon's dad, Chester Davis, was a gruff, phlegm-spitting, profane tough nut to crack. Mr. Davis practiced law and was a key advisor to his "special" client—the reclusive Howard Hughes.

At the start of our freshman Christmas vacation, Jon called. Out of the blue, he was expected to join his parents onboard Chester's private jet the following day. They were going to Grand Bahama for eight days. This was conveyed to him the evening before their departure, and he bristled at the thought of spending the bulk of his vacation with his parents, without any friends or his beloved horses on the farm. His call was to invite me to join him.

I had already made a few plans for the week and told him that there was no way I could afford a trip to Rhode Island, let alone a week-long vacation in the Caribbean. "No worries," Jon said, "we have an extra seat on the plane. We'll have a blast. My dad has some business on the island and the entire cost is being expensed. We'll have the run of the place. C'mon, Ralph," he pleaded. Hmmm, I thought, how could I deny Jon the pleasure of my company? Once I had my parents' consent, I eagerly packed a suitcase and, early the next morning, outside a private hangar at the nearby Westchester Airport, I rendezvoused with Jon and his parents by a gleaming private Learjet. I never asked whether the jet was Mr. Davis's or if Hughes had provided it for Chester's frequent flights to meet with the famous recluse. Once fully refueled, we were off. The one stewardess offered me a mimosa which I politely turned down. Chester insisted and I relented. Nothing like drinking at 9 a.m. at thirty thousand feet to help lose your inhibition.

The week went by quickly and we indeed had a great time, snorkeling by day and drinking by night. We stayed at the luxurious Xanadu Beach Resort and Marina which had recently been renovated following its sale to a company created by Mr. Davis for the benefit of Hughes. At several points during the week, when we were sitting at the poolside bar or tanning on our beach chairs, Jon would point to a penthouse window, which was generally kept shrouded by dark curtains. Finally, on our last look, we got a glimpse of the hotel's famous owner who was meeting with Mr. Davis. Howard Hughes had been in the news recently over an unauthorized and fraudulent autobiography purportedly ghost written by Clifford Irving. It seemed that Mr. Davis was playing some kind of fixer role for Hughes, but I didn't dare ask Jon.

During my second ninth grade, I became a contributing citizen of Wilbraham Academy. To be sure, I didn't suddenly become an angel or an ideal student, but I recognized the need to turn myself around and that to do so, I would need to make some serious changes. I wasn't sure I could succeed. However, because of my New York upbringing, and through a process of osmosis, I was more cosmopolitan than most of my peers at the Academy, and that boosted my self-esteem.

More than half of Wilbraham students were from within 15 miles of the school, which meant that their access to culture and its rewards was limited to the bland fare provided by a few Springfield arts organizations. Knowledge that I took for granted was a revelation to my classmates. For example, my proximity to Broadway and off-Broadway helped to feed my knowledge of and interest in theater, as did my visits to some of the world's best museums.

In the same vein, I loved music, and I had very broad, catholic tastes that stretched from bebop jazz and atonal classical to British folk. I had an unusual ability to recall not only artists and their work, needing only a few notes to identify obscure songs, but also the minutiae of sidemen, producers, and record label execs. This group of seemingly disparate people crisscrossed and overlapped in ways that I could see in my mind's eye, as if I were the Nobel Prize–winning mathematician, John Forbes Nash.

The various arts-driven confidence boosters—attributable to the accident of my New York address—were in and of themselves not enough to complete my academic turnaround. That would require interaction with Nick Fleck, my singular English teacher.

Mr. Fleck was like no one I had ever met. He was unconventional in both the content and style of his teaching. He would sit with his right leg tucked under his left thigh. He wore moss-green fatigues and faded brown safari shirts, complete with epaulets and the faded outlines of excised shoulder pads. When he was excited, he would run his fingers through the crown of his hair in a circular motion and exclaim, "Yes, that's it!" or "No, are you serious?" Mr. Fleck's penchant for, and willingness to provide personally tailored learning "programs" was made possible by the Academy's attractive student-teacher ratio. In short order, he was able to assess our individual weaknesses and strengths, and our potential on an academic, social, and moral basis. He abhorred a mind that didn't take risks.

Fleck believed everyone has a well of creativity which, when accessed and nurtured, leads to satisfaction and a sense of productivity. But while that was easily said, it was difficult to accomplish. How could he help evince that creativity? He began by assigning us writing homework that had no resemblance to other classes we might have taken. Here are two typically Fleckian exercises:

- What is the opposite of a tree? Define, describe, and provide an opinion of its utility.
- Write a description of your left hand as if you were doing so for the benefit of a blind man who has never "seen" before.

Fleck loved the concept of figure/ground, whereby the relationship of the foreground object to its background is not stable. A simple example might be a line drawing of the profiles of twins looking at one another. Those two profiles have as their background the interior space between them. But on closer inspection that interior space looks like a candle holder, and therefore the foreground and interior space have switched places. Fleck had us discuss the concept and its use among surrealists, notably Salvador Dalí, and the 1962 short movie adaptation of the Ambrose Bierce story, *Occurrence at Owl Creek Bridge*.

Fleck was also my JV soccer coach that first year, and he continued to be very supportive of me, which gave me courage to reach for improvement in other classes such as algebra and chemistry, whose answers were not at all intuitive to me. I looked up to Nick and spent much time with his family, especially as I became one of the Flecks' go-to babysitters.

On balance, my first year at Wilbraham was quite positive, but I missed my friends and family. I began to spend weekends in Scarsdale and devoted most of my time there to enjoying the company of several friends, particularly Rob Blashek and Ken Rothstein. All three of us went to Camp Takajo but it wasn't until I left Scarsdale High School that I became very friendly with Ken. Generally upbeat, his personality traits ran the gamut. He was very entertaining and had a silly streak. Much to my embarrassment, he had no compunction about approaching celebrities and getting their autographs. He was rarely on time for dinner or other scheduled dates. The two of us were nearly always on the same wavelength, particularly with our criticism of various cultural, societal and even gastronomic trends, personalities, and works.

Kenny was both a stand-up comedian and a sometimes-gifted impressionist. The latter role enabled him to transform himself into any of a long roster of personalities, from Moms Mabley to

Humphrey Bogart, and from Howard Cosell and Ed Sullivan to Julia Child. Like me, he was enamored with the quality of Jewish humor and its place in the history of comedy. Prior to the Soon-Yi outrage, we both marveled at Woody Allen's ability as writer, lead actor, and director of a few of the finest comic films ever made. While not part of a movie, "The Moose" skit from Woody's masterful live stand-up show double LP remains an unparalleled accomplishment that to this day we both quote from liberally.

Aware that I was now at an all-boys prep school, Rob and Ken attempted to provide me with dates when I was back home. Ken's then-girlfriend, Lisa, was very attractive, with raven hair and perfectly painted bright red nails. She had a delicate china doll look and was shy around me. She was from nearby Larchmont and had a trace of Brooklyn in her speech, giving me a false heuristic impression that she was not intelligent. Regardless, she was very sweet and definitely hot. We got along quite well, and when I got off my holier-than-thou throne, I had to admit that she was quite pleasant to be around. Lucky Ken was punching above his weight.

Lisa proposed a plan one evening. If Ken and I agreed to it, she would have her older sister, Gina, join us as my date. The four of us ended up in a large and softly foliated woods. It was a warm spring night, the moon nearly full and the sky crystal clear and littered with stars. Once again, I was in that same movie where I was expected to take charge, but didn't feel I had the requisite control of the situation. But then Lisa went to her sister and whispered something. Before I knew it, her sister Gina had taken Ken's hand for a walk deeper into the woods—and sweet Lisa had her tongue down my throat.

Rob and I also had a few interesting evenings together in search of girls. These included a dance at New Rochelle's Glen Island Casino, on whose beach Rob worked as a summer lifeguard. After a few strolls around the perimeter of the dance floor, I determined there was no one there that held my interest. Just as I was telling Rob we should leave, I caught a glimpse of *her*. She was the it girl for me. She was wearing tight-fitting jeans and a halter top, and had long, sandy blonde hair, a knockout figure, and a radiant smile.

Rob saw me staring at her and began to insist that I ask her to dance. I wasn't sure I had the gumption to be that bold, but then I saw that she was looking at me. Was I the reason she was smiling? Couldn't be, but… then again, she was still smiling at me. I took a deep breath and walked across the crowded dance floor, where she waited on the edge. Now I could see her beautiful soft blue eyes. I opened my mouth and clumsily asked, "Do you dance?" "Do I *whaaat*? Of course I dance," she brayed in the loudest, most nasal voice I had ever heard. We had one dance, and I left with Rob, disappointed at the outcome but pleased I had found some courage that night.

There were several others, but the one who would stick for a while was Patti Lynch, the redheaded, freckled-faced daughter of a NYC policeman. Patti was fun-loving and very much at ease with who she was. We dated for a few months of my freshman year and had some memorable evenings, including one when we joined Rob and our friend Debbie Burke to see Crosby, Stills, Nash & Young during their *4-Way Street* tour.

I really liked Patti. I adored her perfume (Taboo, I believe) but still moved slowly, putting Patti on a proverbial pedestal. Shortly after we split up, our friend Bruce Black dated Patti and

I heard that he went further with her in their first week than I had in our six months together.

I returned to Wilbraham after the summer break, gung-ho for my sophomore year. Wilbraham was not the same place that I had left in early June.

First off, Monson, another nearby private school, had agreed to merge into the Academy. The result was a modest bump in our student numbers and a change of the school's name to Wilbraham Monson Academy. This had virtually no impact on me or Wilbraham. From what I could see there were no changes in our facilities, and I can't imagine that Monson had much of an endowment, likely relying on its annual campaigns for a high percentage of its operating budget. I suspect that Monson was struggling financially and, instead of closing outright, opted to realize the value of its land and donor list via the merger.

The more meaningful change was that WMA became co-ed on that first day of school. The process of achieving full parity between the sexes and integrating the girls into the school's culture would be very deliberate and take several years. In its initial year the first coeds made for a small group of incoming freshmen. The odds were in their favor: 18 girls to about 200 boys.

Now that I was back from summer recess, I was surprised by how much I missed the Academy, and the wonderful array of characters who were in my circle. These included Tim Platt and James Downey.

Tim was raised in Fort Worth and had the lazy drawl to prove it. His deep, sonorous singing voice was much better than average, and he got by on guitar. He favored Willie Nelson and would sing the outlaw's lyrics:

Shotgun Willie sits around in his underwear
Biting on a bullet and pulling all of his hair
Shotgun Willie's got all of his family there

I spent a week with Tim in Texas during a stretch of scorching Fort Worth weather in which every day was at or over 100 degrees. I was thrilled to be the guest rhythm guitarist and drummer in Tim's local pick-up band. Thankfully, our sessions at a hall at the local VFW hall were not recorded.

James Downey was another boarding student who came from nearby Longmeadow. Prior to Wilbraham, James had attended school at Portsmouth Abbey and School in Rhode Island. Founded in the 1920s, this Benedictine-rooted school is sited on the shores of Narragansett Bay. As a teenager James' pasty face was pale with blotches of muted red. He recalled the Irish Troubles. Moreover, until he grew into his face, its features seemed to be placed individually, like a real-life Mr. Potato head or a Cubist-style portrait. But to me and all who knew him, James was as beautiful as they come. I had never, nor would I ever, meet anyone so sweet, thoughtful and caring as James. He would feature in several key scenes of my Wilbraham years.

Of the nineteen trailblazing girls, there were only a few I initially set out to meet. Cathy Clark was the younger sister of Tim Clark, a classmate of mine. The entire Clark family were avid skiers, including Cathy. Fresh, freckle-faced Cathy had a great smile that made her already narrow eyes turn to slits. She was tomboyish and liked to have fun. My roommate, Jon, confided to me that he "liked" Cathy. Until any coupling became a reality, he would mope around the school with his head hanging down.

Chris Galavotti was the girl I had my eye on. She often wore her lustrous dark hair parted down the middle and her chocolate brown eyes were very expressive. I thought she was very attractive and, as I got to know her, extremely intelligent with a big appetite for learning. While Chris was more serious than the other girls, she had an appreciation for humor, an important trait for me. Chris's mix of beauty, intellectual substance, and laughter bewitched me and by the Thanksgiving break, I, too, was in (puppy) love.

Our close-knit group now included the two girls and would come to accommodate several others, including Pat Booker, Lisa Montoro and Sally Tower. We would meet at the Rez, where we discussed our teachers, courses, and the greater world "outside." The Rez was generally thought to be student-only turf, safe from the judging eyes of faculty. This meant that anyone was free to light up a joint and smoke with impunity. I rarely did, because I generally disliked pot's effect on me. Drinking beer was fine, and over the course of our sophomore year, Jon and I "decorated" our room with glued-on, wall-to-wall empty beer cans. We must have used over 500 cans. Although this was a thumb in the eyes of the faculty, by the time we undertook this project, Jon and I were viewed as class leaders—and with that came some perks and a tacit loosening of the leash. Another advantage to our informal elevated status was the administration's approval of my request to bring my car on campus. Our group was now mobile.

On James's invitation, we planned to stay over one Saturday night at his family's underutilized country house in the small hamlet of Washington, Massachusetts. The town was in upper Hampshire County, close to the southeast border of Berkshire County. We met outside the WMA dining hall in the late afternoon when the winter sun was setting. We were a party of seven. Besides me and James, there was Chris, Cathy, Jon, Pat, and Tim. James had also been given the okay to have his automobile on campus and together the two of us went to retrieve our cars in long-term parking across from the field house. Light flakes of snow began to fall. I sensed a slight shift in the balance of our group. As the others figured out how they would split up for the ride, I thought there was a current running through Tim, Cathy, and Jon. Maybe it was nothing.

Chris got in my car, as did Tim. James drove Cathy, Pat, and Jon. Onward we went, as the snow continued to fall and intensify. We stopped near Washington at a liquor store and loaded up. Due to the weather, the ride took longer than usual. I was relieved to have nearly completed the journey without incident. For the final leg of our ride the snow accelerated. My knuckles were as white as the blinding snow. The now-dangerous weather had me dispirited. I had no jokes at the ready or stories to tell. Chris and Tim felt this and remained silent. But then, at last, we were face to face with James Downey's 1894 Colonial-style home.

The house was perfect, even though it took some time for us to make a fire and begin to warm up. It was a quintessential center-entrance antique Colonial with a classic configuration. From a small entranceway, visitors could go left into a music room, right into the living room, or straight—either up the central stairs to the second floor or down the hallway just ahead and to the side of the stairs. This central hallway led to the kitchen, a guest bathroom, and the back portion of the house, which included a remote bedroom suite and an office that could also serve as a small bedroom. The trio of bedrooms on the second floor included the master, which had an en suite bathroom, and another bathroom shared by the other two bedrooms.

The music room was dominated by a large tapestry that depicted two women walking by a river. A fireplace was situated opposite the grand piano, an old Yamaha, somewhat distressed and unsurprisingly out of tune, given its exposure to extreme changes in temperatures. Opposite the piano were three chairs with pillows displaying a Dutch petit-point scene. The living room was an amply sized rectangle, anchored by a well-worn sofa across from another fireplace. This room also had a separate sitting area, defined by two plush chairs placed side by side, across from a small green velour settee. Entering further into the living room led to the recently refurbished kitchen and mudroom, which boasted a newly acquired oven and refrigerator.

Because we were behind schedule, we compressed our planned activities into short bursts. Dinner was overseen by Cathy, Pat, and James, but soon Jon and Tim were in the kitchen. Chris and I set up drinks and offered them around. The dinner was a modest offering of spaghetti and meatballs with garlic bread and a simple garden salad. We had also ordered three Fribbles to go. James's two bottles of Chianti Classico were polished off before the spaghetti was all eaten.

After dinner and a dessert of apple pie and Friendly's vanilla ice cream, we played charades and drank vodka, tequila, and bourbon. The charades game required a lack—or suspension—

of self-consciousness. Not easy, particularly for Jon. However, this was in my comfort zone, as I liked acting out, in an exaggerated way, the game titles scrawled on scraps of paper and handed to me by the opposing team. Chris, who this time wasn't on my side, picked up on my approach and did the same. However, the game devolved into side conversations and more drinking. This, in turn, led several of us to become less inhibited.

I found myself on the living room sofa but can't recall clearly when the coupling with Chris began. Chris wanted more privacy and took my hand to lead me to the small bedroom suite in the back of the house. I like to think I was the aggressor, but I don't think so. We were two innocents fumbling with our mutual infatuation. It was thrilling to be together after all these months of longing. Despite my discomfort lying on the sofa and then on the bed in the downstairs suite, and a growing lower pain caused by a case of teenage blue balls, I vowed silently to stay put atop Chris or spooned next to her throughout the night. I didn't want to risk breaking the glorious spell we were under. Even the dissonance caused by Jon's moaning wouldn't seep through to taint the new reality that Chris and I were a couple.

Fittingly, Bob Dylan's just-released *New Morning* album was on the turntable with the auto-replay function enabled throughout the night. After sunrise, I learned that Cathy had followed Tim to the small study-bedroom, leaving Jon wailing for a long time before trudging upstairs for a few hours of fitful sleep. Wasn't Tim aware of Jon's adoration of Cathy? Couldn't he see what he was doing to Jon? In the aftermath of that momentous evening, Jon would declare his feelings to Cathy—who, as it turned out, reciprocated them. Jon would need time to forgive Tim, and he never did so in full.

Chris and I were together for four years. Over the course of our relationship, we supported one another as we matured emotionally and intellectually. Even when we traveled to a clinic in Pelham, NY to end an early pregnancy, Chris remained one of my closest confidants, and my only lover. We were from vastly different backgrounds. She was raised in Wilbraham, not more than a mile from the Academy. Her father Lou was a travelling salesman for a few industrial manufacturers. It was a hard way to earn a living, and he battled a tendency to drink too much, which worried Chris. Her mother, an avid crossword puzzle solver, was a homemaker raising the Galovattis' three daughters and one son. They lived modestly in their modest split-level ranch house and were a relatively happy family.

Chris excelled at school and graduated with my class in three years. She thought she might like to be a writer and was flattered when my family's neighbor, Bob Bernstein—CEO of the venerable publisher Random House—vigorously complimented her on a few pieces, including a favorite poem of mine that she had written. She effortlessly became attached to my Scarsdale friends who had by now spent several weekends visiting us at the Academy. Likewise, Chris had become quite comfortable spending time with my family, both on weekends during the school year and in the summers on Martha's Vineyard.

We discussed the pros and cons of applying to the same college but decided we should each pursue our own experience. We planned to see each other every other weekend. Chris accepted the offer from Hampshire College in Amherst, and I signed on for Trinity in Hartford. There could not have been two more contrasting schools. Hampshire was a new, experimental college. Instead of traditional dorms, most students lived in donut-shaped structures. The scholastic side of Trinity was comparatively formal, traditional. Likewise, Trinity's Greek houses dominated social life. At Hampshire, you were on your own to find—or create—your entertainment, activism campaign, and so on.

Once, when I was visiting Chris, an unnerving, loud alarm went off at 2:30 a.m. It was difficult to ascertain what was happening. Students, just roused from sleep, covered their unbrushed mouths to avoid being tagged as a sour breath. They patted down their bed hair. The confusion ended when someone yelled, "It's been hit! Quick, to the gym." We could have returned to our room, but we forged ahead, and when we arrived at 2:45 a.m., we saw that the giant bubble that served as the roof of Hampshire's massive gymnasium had been macheted by an inconsolable sophomore from Donut Twelve. His boyfriend had jilted him, and he apparently needed to destroy something. For the next three hours, we watched the bubble slowly deflate. My kind of fun!

Before we matriculated, we had the summer to enjoy. For part of it, Chris and I worked together as teachers in Farmington, CT, on the campus of Miss Porter's School for Girls. Miss Porter's was known as an elite prep school, a finishing school with high standards and academic rigor. Each June, its idyllic campus was taken over by a program that provided special classes to poor, inner-city teenage girls from Hartford's worst neighborhoods. My friend John Fitzgerald, who also happened to be entering Hampshire College in the fall, taught an English class with me.

Our students were girls of color, nearly all Black and a few Latinas. Their ages ranged from thirteen to sixteen. Of the twenty-one students in our class, six of them were mothers or currently pregnant. The girls were wary, unruly, and utterly disinterested in our class.

When it became clear that teaching from standard-fare lesson plans would be futile, John and I changed tactics. As the girls shuffled into the classroom the next morning in their usual disruptive manner, we let blast a foghorn, getting their attention for at least a moment. I stood and asked facetiously if anyone had ever read a book. One or two brave girls quietly assented. Then I looked around the room and asked if anyone had ever written a book. They jeered me in unison. Of course they hadn't written a book.

"Listen up," John said. "We are quite serious. Starting now, our goal is to have each of you contribute to the writing of a book whose plot, characters, and title will be provided by the class." The girls weren't sure what to make of our midcourse turn, and a few responded with the kind of negativism that had plagued us from the start. I pointed out that by following our lead, we would abandon the dry and dreaded English primer that was inflexibly tethered to their class syllabus.

We peremptorily posed a few questions, hoping to get at least some of the class to participate and kickstart our project. What happens in the book? What is the story line? Who are the main characters? How do they respond to adversity? What are their good and bad traits? The class looked at me as if I were an alien. Still, there was only a low-level buzz in the room. Over the hum of classroom chatter, JoJo shouted: "It's about DeVaughn Inwood and his lady Mo'esha. And how they have this dream about leaving the projects. But the dream is too hard to get to—it isn't real, that possibility to succeed."

I was delighted. JoJo, a smart but behaviorally difficult student, was a leader among her classmates. She had cracked open the cool of writing. For the next three weeks, every weekday the girls offered their descriptions, plot twists, and character sketches for our tome-to-be. With two days left in the program, we had completed 48 typewritten pages. John and I had 25 copies printed and spiral bound. We even displayed a few morsels from the "critics" on the title page. One critic effused that the book "takes you to the depths of despair… and leaves you there." Another simply stated, "I wept!" The girls ripped into the cartons of books. It was all so very satisfying—for me and John, and more importantly, for the girls.

During a brief break in July, Rob Blashek and I attended the mud bath that was the Watkins Glen Summer Music Festival. This was for Woodstock wannabe folks like the two of us. Despite the wonderful music—which featured The Grateful Dead, The Allman Brothers, and the Band—I was a little too uptight to get into the free love spirit and nervous about being with 650,000 of my closest friends in the pouring rain. Still, I wore the weekend retreat as a badge of honor.

I then attended summer school at Andover in northern Massachusetts. I had signed up to take an intensive film course, which to my pleasant surprise was taught by the grandson of one of the Marx brothers. Marx's knowledge of film was encyclopedic as was his understanding of film techniques. Some of my favorite films of all time were screened, including the silent *Sunrise*, *La Strada*, *Citizen Kane*, *Black Orpheus*, *The Bicycle Thief*, and of course, the Marx Brothers' *Night at the Opera*. For our own mini-film, we constructed a 14-foot track upon which a dolly carried our camera for a long moving shot. I also taught a not-for-credit course on the Beach Boys, focusing on the band's less commercial records of their "middle period" including *Carl and the Passions, Sunflower, Holland,* and *Surf's Up!* Apparently, any ego issues that may have kept me from taking on an authoritative role were in the past.

Attending these weekly "classes" were my new friends Rory Kessler and David Friendly. David was a smart, warm-hearted, and articulate guy. His father was Fred Friendly, the revered producer of broadcaster Edward R. Murrow. I can assure you that David's father bore no resemblance to George Clooney, who portrays him in the Broadway version of *Good Night, and Good Luck*.

Rory was raised in Lake Success, near the Five Towns on Long Island. She was an attractive brunette with wavy hair and a very curvy figure. She wanted badly to fall in love and hoped that her love for me would be reciprocated. Rory was the daughter of a successful jingle writer who wrote a catchy tune for Coca Cola. As much as I delighted in her attention, I still placed a value on my commitment to Chris—even as that commitment was fraying with the realization that the two of us would be going separate ways after our graduation from Wilbraham. After several months, I had to let Rory down, a decision I regretted.

Chris and I continued as a couple, but the cracks were deepening. I tried to maintain our plan to visit each other two weekends a month, but our priorities were shifting. I was beginning to enjoy new friends on campus, while Chris had fallen for an über-intellectual, bisexual man from New York City. This was initially hard on me, and I fought against it. After several weeks, however, I was able to regain perspective and realized that, in the words of *Casablanca*'s Rick Blaine, "the problems of three little people don't amount to a hill of beans in this crazy world." We were fortunate to have made positive contributions to each other's growth over the last several years. So, with a few tears in our eyes, we walked away from one another—even as we counted our blessings for the years we had shared.

Chapter 4

Ancora Tu

Fall had arrived at Trinity, and a sense of freshness and hope dusted the campus. The colors of the sky were intensely vivid, from azure to royal blue. Even on ashy, overcast days, dramatic gray cumulus compositions felt dangerously pregnant with advancing storms. The cloud formations seemed to hover uneasily very low on the horizon, as if descending to earth to warn us.

I lived in Elton, which faced Jones, another mostly freshman dormitory. In between the two buildings was a snug courtyard that led to the college's main dining facilities. My roommate was Jim Fairbrother who, despite his decision to transfer to Wesleyan at year's end, would remain a very close friend. During freshman orientation, Jim and I began the process of identifying potential friends. This was aided by the freshman class directory, better known in those pre-woke days as the "Pig Book." It contained individual black-and-white headshots of the entire freshman class along with their hometowns and dorm assignments. The distribution of the book broke down much of the reticence that restricted conversation among groups of freshmen. What better way to loosen up new arrivals to campus than to discuss or grade those little black-and-white pictures in the directory?

There were several girls whose pictures piqued my interest. Katie Philson and Meredith Dixon—attractive, preppy blondes—were strangers to me, yet when I looked at their pictures, I sensed a previous connection with both. While Meredith and Katie went to Miss Porter's, that was incidental and not the reason I recognized them. It took me a frustrating amount of time before I recalled where I had previously seen these two and under what circumstances.

In 1970, Wilbraham Monson Academy had asked the Yippie activist and member of the Chicago Seven, Jerry Rubin to speak to the entire academy. In addition, students from several other private schools were invited to attend—including Merideth and Katie. The traditional podium-facing seating arrangement was eschewed in favor of an in-the-round configuration. As a result, when audience members were looking at Rubin, they couldn't help but see others seated behind him. From my vantage point, just off Rubin's left shoulder, I could see Meredith and Katie and they could see me. It was a game. Who would get caught staring at whom? How quickly would we refocus our gaze on Rubin?

How could I not remember them!

At Trinity, I became good friends with both Katie and Meredith. We spent time together in New York City on school breaks, going to concerts and, on Christmas eve, midnight mass at St. Patrick's Cathedral. Katie was always great company. Meredith had a tough-gal veneer and a very dry sense of humor—a combination I thoroughly enjoyed.

The third blonde girl from the class directory was Nancy Wolfson, with whom I had a very complex relationship. Her snapshot captured not only Nancy's beauty but also an inscrutable coolness. Her face was open and expressive, and she could be arch in her manner. Nancy was open to new experiences and took my cultural suggestions seriously, especially those regarding music. Over our four years at Trinity, including our junior year abroad studying in Rome and for several years beyond, we were extremely close, the best of friends. Fittingly, my inability to learn more than 30–50 phrases in Italian earned me the nickname "the crazy American." By contrast, Nancy won the Italian Prize and was fluent in both the language and the culture's modes of behavior.

Our ability to communicate with Italians without misunderstanding was a marvel—but this didn't apply when it came to expressing the feelings we had for each other. We loved each other, but generally didn't act on those feelings. Nancy and I were victims of poor timing. We had a mutual habit of recognizing what was staring us in the face just as the other was starting a new relationship and had become unavailable. This was true even in the final week before my wedding, when Nancy suggested I reconsider, or at least take more time before marrying Amy.

My course load was ambitious, but I thought I could stretch intellectually. Hume, Hegel, Bellow, Pasolini, Maslow, Harriman, Erikson, Amis, Proust, Caravaggio, Melville, and Thomas Aquinas were a few of the personalities I met while attending my classes and completing the assigned readings. Given my imperfect study habits, I was pleased to survive my biggest deficit—my tendency to fall behind in my homework— and still do well on papers and final exams. On more than one occasion, I had to pull consecutive all-nighters, from which I needed time to recover.

In my first year of college, I was a joiner. I became the starting left forward for Trinity's JV soccer team. We were Division Three, part of the New England Small College Athletic Conference (NESCAC), and our competition included Amherst, Tufts, Williams, Bowdoin, Colby, and Middlebury. We had a winning but unremarkable season, although I could look back proudly on my tying goal against the much-revered Williams team.

The next summer, while wading at the beach in Narragansett Bay, a wave seemed to gently kiss my knee—but it was enough to cause my collapse. This occurred before the widespread use of arthroscopic surgery. The painful ACL procedure that followed ended my competitive collegiate athletic life and required over four months of recovery. My sweet brother Michael was pressed into service to hold up my leg whenever I needed to go to the bathroom. I gave him one of my Takajo purple turtles for going above and beyond the call of duty.

The silver lining to my knee injury was that the time I no longer needed for soccer enabled me to deeply commit to WRTC-FM, Trinity's radio station. Beyond my twice-weekly three-hour show, I became involved in the administrative and operational nuts and bolts of the station. This meant learning the station's finances and understanding the tools our engineers used to maintain and extend its reach. I spent hours every day listening to new and obscure music to share with my program's listeners.

My ascension to Program Director was never impeded by other serious candidates. From my perch as PD, I began aggressively contacting publicity and promotion executives at music companies, hoping to increase the number and quality of interviewees made available to WRTC. Musicians I interviewed ranged from a then little-known Bruce Springsteen to Hall & Oates, NRBQ, Eric Andersen, and Jonathan Edwards.

Sadly, I have no idea where the tape is from my brief talk with the Boss. We had our sit-down following his show in October 1974 at the Sanderson Theater in Springfield, which soon after was rechristened the Paramount Theater. Rob and Ken were lucky enough to catch Bruce's show at Brown the previous year, and like millions of others, we all followed the trajectory of his stardom and artistry.

The station had its own set of characters, as well as a culture unlike anything else on campus. The airwaves were turned over to a series of Black DJs every night from 10 p.m. to 2 a.m. Their shows mixed soul, jazz, spoken word, and even advice for the lovelorn. On weekend mornings, the station programming slots were geared toward Hartford's large Portuguese community.

Aside from these specialty shows, WRTC was at heart a blues, R&B, rock, and folk station. My good friend Tony Schaefer had a show that followed mine in the late afternoon. Tony's hold on—and love of—music was intense and infectious. He was great to be around, and we had the joy of riding down to Miami Beach together one spring break. We stayed with my paternal grandmother, who seemed to take to Tony's good manners. Tony's mother was the attractive and youthful life partner of Tony's dad, the Chairman of Kravco. The company was a leader in the development and management of very large upscale malls, including the first of its kind: King of Prussia, outside Philadelphia.

I was also happily befriended by Howard Goldstein, who was remarkably self-reliant despite his blindness. We often crossed paths at the radio station or upstairs on the edge of the quad. Howard let me take his arm and walk him to wherever he needed to go—usually to the end of the long walkway beside the ivied buildings, where I'd see him into his dorm entranceway. He had a great sense of humor and enough blind-man jokes to fill in any gaps when he sensed the conversation with his classmates was flagging.

The following year, I rented an apartment off-campus on nearby School Street with my friend Larry Glassman. Larry had been on my floor in Elton and was paired, during our freshman year, with Jim Graves of Wilmington, DE, a hopeless romantic who I first ran into while he was watching the treacly *Love Story* with tears streaming down his cheeks. Larry hailed from Long Island and was one of the calmest people I knew. This was particularly true after he smoked a joint, completed his exercise regimen, or meditated for 20 minutes. The cynic in me dismissed Larry's mindfulness routines as new-age pap, but I longed to learn how to be more centered and to let go of my self-consciousness. Larry managed the stress of his grueling pre-med program quite well. He would go on to become a highly regarded thoracic surgeon at Long Island Jewish Hospital.

Our upstairs neighbors were Bill Metz and Elihu Rubin. Bill and Elihu would often come down for dinner or just to hang out with me and Larry. I liked them both and spent increasing amounts of time with Elihu. He was well-read on the subjects that mattered to him most, particularly Judaism in America and its cultural achievements. Elihu's worldview was informed by fiercely liberal Jewish sources, from *Tikkun* and *The Forward* to WBAI-FM.

Elihu was from Bayside, Queens, and his father was a senior

compounding chemist for the groundbreaking Fifth Avenue dermatologist, Norman Orentreich. We spent time in the East Village, and he liked to point out historically important spots that had since been decimated by time and neglect. While in the neighborhood, we often enjoyed egg creams from the Gem Spa, which were perfect refreshers. Intellectually enigmatic, Elihu was assertive in his arguments and drawn to sources that were anything but mainstream. It was easy to view him as a curmudgeon; indeed, I think he created his grumpy persona on purpose. But his friends knew that there was no greater sweetheart of a guy.

Elihu helped me recapture my affinity for Jewish history and culture. Even so, Trinity was not Yeshiva, and during that sophomore year, I was rushed by the elite and extremely Waspy fraternity, St. Anthony's Hall. St. A's was located on Summit Street, at the top of the highest elevation in Hartford, which was said to be the site of witch hangings in the late 17th century.

The Hall was unique among the Greek houses in that its chapter house appeared to have two floors. But by getting access to the turret's internal cone—available only by key and with written approval by either the #1 or the #2—and climbing its winding steps, the old building offered up a secret floor and a darkly candlelit meeting room. Meetings were held on Wednesday evenings. We brothers would dress in suits and ties for dinner, while our female dining club guests also dressed in relatively formal garb. Once our meal and post-dinner drinks were finished, we would say our good evenings to the women and march off to the chapter house without them.

There, we accessed the turret and, in a darkened changing room, donned our cowled black robes and filed into the secret meeting room. At the special sign—index finger held pointing up to the tip of the nose, moved forward about six inches, and then drawn back to just above the lips—we would reciprocate these motions first to the #1 and then to the #2. Finally seated, we were ready to... perform!

Unbeknownst to the rest of the student body, St. Anthony's was a literary club of sorts. Each week, one or more brothers would tell a story, review a book, read original poetry, or do whatever the spirit moved him to do. One Wednesday evening early in my St. A's membership, I teamed up with Tim Ghriskey, whose abstract, richly colorful photographs were beautiful compositions. I added my DJ song selections and editing abilities and somehow the photographs and music supported and improved each other. When I became the #1, Tim took on the #2 role. Our paths would remain interwoven for the next several decades.

To be clear, St. A's wasn't only engaged in highbrow activities. The regular Thursday Night Club was more in line with the insanity of any frat party one can imagine. I often hung out with John Battle during these loud affairs. John was my senior by a year and one of my favorite people at Trinity. He was a lady killer, with jet-black hair and dark eyes made for brooding—but he was having too much fun with life and could smile for an entire evening. When he was 14, John spent time living in Egypt during the 1967 Arab-Israeli War. His father was the U.S. Ambassador to Egypt, and John's family was given the use of a very commodious house in Cairo with a staff at their disposal.

In early 1976, while I was in my junior year at Trinity, my mother, reference librarian extraordinaire, sent me a very short, jolting news clipping. Mom was aware of my ongoing interest in Camp Takajo and the wunderkind John Edgar Wideman, son-in-law of camp owner Morty Goldman. The article recounted a botched robbery and murder that had taken place in Homewood, a neighborhood in Pittsburgh that had seen better days. It reported that three fugitives were on the run and were finally captured by police in Wyoming. Included in the trio was Robby Wideman, John's youngest brother who was arrested as an accessory to murder. Robby had been involved in a botched robbery and although he never shot the victim he was still convicted and given a life sentence.

What followed was a re-stranding of the Wideman brothers' shared DNA. John made clear his sense of guilt at abandoning his family—and his Blackness. In his memoir *Brothers and Keepers*, John posits a good seed/bad seed dialectic, with Robby embodying badness and John representing the good seed. But for John, the simplicity of that construct was itself a flaw. In a letter to John, his brother quotes the Sly Stone song "Family Affair":

> *One child grows up to be somebody*
> *who just loved to learn*
> *And the other grows up to be*
> *somebody who just loves to burn*
> *Mom loves the both of them*
> *you see it in the blood*
> *Both kids are good to Mom*
> *blood thicker than the mud*
> *It's a family affair*

I was deeply invested in the Wideman-Goldman clan. Ever

since meeting Morty as a pre-teen and being so taken with his principled gravitas and his warm, kind sincerity, I had attached to Morty and his family an ideal that was both naïve and unfair. To my simplistic, optimistic thinking, this mixed-race, well-educated family represented the promise of '60s liberalism. Over time, that promise would become skewed, mutate, and decay regardless of how this family navigated a more dangerous and complex world. I was growing up and beginning to see the world more for what it was, rather than as I had simply, non-critically hoped it would be.

This shift began as I read Wideman's memoir *Brothers and Keepers*. In one minor side story, John writes about a black-and-white Sony TV that was stolen from his and Judy's house. The TV had been a gift from his father-in-law, Morty, who later also bought a replacement for them. John submitted an insurance claim and dismissed Judy's suggestion that he specify the proceeds should go directly to Morty.

At around this time, Robby confessed that he had taken the TV and hocked it at a nearby pawn shop. He was strung out and needed money to score drugs, desperate to quell the addiction's roar in his head.

At a Goldman family gathering with Morty and his wife Elise months later, the theft of the TV came up in conversation. John reported offhandedly that the insurance company had recently paid off the claim so that he had come out well. In that moment, too late to walk back his words let alone his actions, John realized that the insurance money should clearly have gone directly to Morty. From the corner of his eye, he saw the surprise and hurt on his father-in-law's face. In this way, John understood his own failure to Morty. How "selfishly, thoughtlessly, even corruptibly" he had behaved.

It wasn't a failure of premeditation, he wrote, but a failure of instinct. Without the instinct to do the right thing by Morty, John would never be able to distinguish his actions from those of his brother, Robby's. Weren't there two robberies? The theft of the TV and the grab for the insurance money?

Brothers and Keepers is rife with John's self-doubt, guilt, and self-reflection. A piece published in *The Pittsburgh Quarterly*, written by Robby's lawyer Mark Schwartz, described the total disintegration of the attorney's profound awe and admiration for John. In its place grew resentment, even hatred for Wideman. Schwartz points to John's decision to leverage the publicity that would attend the publishing of his acclaimed memoir. Indeed, in a widely viewed *60 Minutes* episode, Wideman did just that.

According to Schwartz, connecting the two brothers was helpful to John and his publisher but backfired on Robby. At Robby's initial parole board meeting—and at similar meetings that took place over the next several decades—John sought to focus the board's attention on the link between the "good seed" and the "bad seed" brothers. However, neither John nor Schwartz firmly established the duality inherent in the family, nor did they articulate the relevance of this distinction on the question of Robby's possible early release. Schwartz had wanted to pursue a more traditional, merits-based approach. According to Schwartz, John's intractable stance cost his younger brother twenty more years of incarceration. After forty-four years, Robby Wideman was finally released and became a free man in 2019.

Still, the Goldman-Wideman family would endure even greater and more violent challenges within just a few years of Robby's initial incarceration.

Part Two

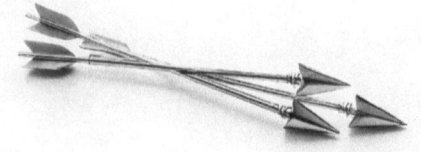

Chapter 5

Swimming Upstream

Senior year was upon me, and as St. Anthony's #1, I had my pick of the fraternity's dorm rooms. With Tim Ghriskey as my roommate, we selected a three-room suite considered, hands-down, the best digs on the entire Trinity campus. Our large bay windows, perched at the highest point in the city, opened onto the small but well-tended quad. It was a terrific spot from which to project Little Feat, Miles Davis, the Allman Brothers, and other uplifting fall and spring music to the many denizens of our mini quad. We gave Tim's Klipsch speakers a workout.

Tim and I were friendly with Margo Halle and Ellen Burchenal, who spent a good amount of time hanging out in our suite. I liked both women—they were attractive, bright, and very thoughtful. They were never overtly flirty and remained above the usual fraternity nonsense, particularly among the women of the St. A's Dining Club. While their unguarded assessments of the St. A's scene were unstinting in their criticism, they were socially facile enough to avoid being seen as malcontents. Like me, Ellen had a family house on Martha's Vineyard, and we were both on the island as it prepared for the filming of Peter Benchley's *Jaws*. That spring, actor Richard Dreyfus made more than one attempt to pick up Ellen from his perch on the bar stools of the Harborside Inn in Edgartown. He was not Ellen's idea of the living end, but she enjoyed toying with him for a few weeks. I was a fan of his performance in the *Apprenticeship of Duddy Kravitz*, so I was happy to have a beer with him on a few occasions.

In the early part of my senior year, my primary goal was to secure a job for the following fall—preferably one that would help launch me on a satisfying and lucrative career. Most of my friends were pursuing MBA or law degrees or entering bank training programs. None of these options appealed to me in the least. At a formal St. A's alumni event that October, I gave a speech to welcome the alumni "brothers" back to the Hall. In it, I quoted liberally from Mel Brooks and Woody Allen without attribution. I felt the irony of entertaining these gentiles with the comedic language of my Jewish people. Regardless of the origin of these jokes, the audience was roaring with uncontrollable, belly-gut laughter. It was heady stuff for me, and I lapped it all up. When my speech was over, as if in a scene from *The Graduate*, four different alumni handed me their business cards and implored me to call them, especially if I needed a job. Plastics, anyone?

These offers were flattering but not helpful, since the sole focus of my nascent job search revolved around my hope and intention to break into the insular entertainment business. My role model was David Geffen, who had founded Asylum Records after a successful tenure as an agent with the storied William Morris Agency. Like all agents at William Morris, you were expected to begin your career in the mailroom and stay there as a runner until you became irreplaceable to one of the agents, who would then anoint you assistant agent. If you were unusually gifted, you might even leapfrog your mentor.

When Geffen left the agency and started his record label, his William Morris clients followed him to Asylum. His artist roster there reflected both Geffen's negotiating skills and his singular ear, which was keenly tuned to what became known as the LA sound. An example is when Geffen "traded" Asylum-signed Poco to Columbia Records, for the recently formed Crosby, Stills, Nash & Young, two of whose members were under contract at Columbia. Poco appeared to be the better bet, given that its sales track record was already established, but the new configuration of CSNY would push the boundaries of harmonic country rock while shifting the alchemy among its members.

After I had made a persistent pest of myself, I succeeded in securing an interview with Ed Khouri, the head of human resources at the William Morris Agency. We had a very good conversation, during which I held my own. Ed warned me about the cutthroat nature of the business and the distasteful personalities to whom I'd be exposed. "No matter," I cried. "I am made of thick skin and will be a contributor to the agency if given the chance." The following week I received a letter from Ed inviting me to join the agency late in the summer of 1977. I was on my way.

Word got out that I had my dream offer in hand. I was gratified that so many friends and family reached out to offer their sincere congratulations. One of the well-wishers was Larry Uttal, my step-uncle by way of my maternal grandmother's second marriage to Larry's father, Henry Uttal. Larry asked me to call his office to set up a meeting as soon as possible.

Larry ran a record company called Private Stock. I would come to call it Private Schlock, due to the company's output of ultra-commercial, Top 40, sometimes cloyingly sweet music. I called his assistant Carol and arranged to see him at his office at 40 West 57th street in New York City. Larry seemed happy to see me; in fact, I noticed that he always seemed happy to see whoever was in front of him. Like nearly all record company execs, Larry had a language of enthusiasm which made it challenging to determine his level of sincerity.

Larry's first career was in the donut business, and he made a success of it. He sold donut machines to commercial and large retail bakeries and did quite well. But Larry didn't envision himself a donut man. Rather, he was smitten with the prospect of becoming a force in the music business. In mid-1950s through the early 1970s, he ran a few record companies that were co-owned by Columbia, including Bell Records and Amy Records. Larry discovered the mega star Barry Manilow, as well as Melissa Manchester and the Partridge Family. He used to send 45s to me and my sister Linda. Most of these made no impression on me, although I was very taken with Alex Chilton's Box Tops song "The Letter" and the Toys' "A Lover's Concerto," which was a "modern" reworking of Christian Petzold's "Minuet in G Major." The song—often mistakenly attributed to Bach—is laden with hooks. It reached number one on the *Cashbox* chart and peaked at number five on the *Billboard* pop chart. Similar success was achieved internationally. Clive Davis consolidated several labels including those for which Larry had been responsible and with his newly acquired catalog and artist roster, launched Arista Records.

Larry invited me to sit down and opened our conversation with a note of disappointment that I hadn't started my search with him and Private Stock. If he had known that I was willing to start in the mail room, he would have offered me a job right then and there. He argued that by starting at his company, I wouldn't need to maneuver to become part of William Morris's music division because, after all, Private Stock was solely a record company.

Looking back at that moment now, I wonder what the arc of my career might have been if I hadn't decided to decline the job offer from William Morris and taken the job at Private Stock. Regardless, I was going to be in the music business once my upcoming summer had run its course.

After graduation in June, I spent time on Martha's Vineyard. I had several friends on the island, including Nancy, Willa Shalit (daughter of the TV arts critic, handlebar-mustachioed Gene Shalit), and Sioux Eagle, with whom I had a brief summer fling. Willa and Nancy were partners in a secondhand clothing store in Edgartown, and Sioux had just opened her own jewelry shop in Vineyard Haven. The clothing store aptly played vintage jazz—songs from another era, many by Billie Holiday and Bessie Smith.

I continued to work in the Edgartown liquor store. Because the island was mostly dry, the two towns that allowed liquor sales became a destination for college students and recent graduates, so I always knew when other friends were "on island." In various combinations, we spent many days and nights on the beach. Sioux enjoyed smoking clove cigarettes, which emitted a sweet, treacly smell and stained her teeth.

Back in NYC, I began my music business career in the Private Stock mailroom, which was thankfully brief. I worked side by side with Carlos, whose older sister oversaw the company's accounts payable, and Van, who was either allergic to showering or had a rare disease that caused a terrible, rotting odor. Carlos was not given to cruelty, but he couldn't help singing the chorus of Lynyrd Skynyrd's "The Smell" whenever Van returned from delivering or picking up whatever was asked of him.

I began spending more and more time with Steve Scharf, the head of A&R (Artist & Repertoire), the department charged with finding and developing talent. A&R functions as the ears of any record company, which is exactly where I wanted to land. I made it clear to Steve that I hoped to become the company's associate director of A&R under his leadership. Steve's office was so cluttered with unopened mail and demo tapes that he enthusiastically invited me to join him that same week to begin the process of sorting through the extensive backlog of submissions.

Steve knew that 99 percent of the unsolicited music pile would be of no interest to Private Stock—or to any record company, for that matter. Even the demos with promise faced an uphill battle because they were unlikely to be the kind of act or song that Private Stock could break commercially. As a result, Steve spent most of his time meeting with agents, music publishers, and producers. His attention to that network paid off periodically. Private Stock had a hit with "A Fifth of Beethoven" by Walter Murphy, a disco version of the maestro's iconic symphony. The song made it onto the soundtrack of the ubiquitous, record-breaking *Saturday Night Fever* from the Robert Stigwood Organization. In turn, Steve's relationship with a key executive at Chappell Music Publishers led to our signing Samantha Sang, whose breathy duet with Barry Gibb, "Emotion," hit number three on the U.S. charts and top five internationally. The "demo" was really a fully produced acetate which only required a fresh remix before pressing—no imagination required.

We also worked with Richard Gottehrer, who produced the debut album from Blondie for us, as well as the first two albums from rockabilly artist Robert Gordon. I was not impressed with the sound of either record but thought his work with Joan Armatrading on *Me Myself I* was solid. Still, it was a long way from Glyn Johns' production on Joan's "Love and Affection."

Private Stock also signed Benny Mardones, whose debut album *Thank God for Girls* was produced by Andrew Loog Oldham, best known as the former manager and producer of the Rolling Stones. Benny was a huge talent, comparable to Steve Perry of Journey. He had one of the best, most soulful voices in the business. His songwriting too often reflected his self-image as an arena rock 'n roller, and he was happiest belting out exuberant, big-build anthems. But it was with his introspective ballads like "Hey Baby" and his breakout hit "Into the Night" that he hushed audiences with the timbre and emotional resonance of his voice. If you want to hear the importance of having a good producer, listen to Benny's first album side by side with his second, *Never Run, Never Hide*, which contains "Into The Night" and was produced by Barry Mraz. Oldham's production pales in comparison to Mraz's.

Benny was a live wire. On its opening day, Benny and I went to an afternoon showing of *Superman* at the Ziegfeld

Theater. After enduring the incessant drip of advertising over its month-long promotional campaign, both of us were excited to be in our seats as the lights went dark. The opening credits soared over our heads and whooshed behind us, heralding the start of something special. Benny—who sometimes sounded like a preacher—stood up on his chair and, at the top of his lungs, yelled "I BELIEVE a man will fly. I BELIEVE a man will fly." Other audience members responded to Benny, shouting, "Yes, I BELIEVE it!"

It wasn't unusual for Benny to stop by my apartment on 10th and University very late in the evening. Music was a nighttime business, and since I wasn't expected into the office until noon, I could get away with a very late night from time to time. However, my roommate and good friend from Scarsdale, Claudia, kept more traditional hours and normally began her day at around 7:45 a.m. For Benny, my apartment might be the last stop on a long evening before heading up to Washington Heights, where he and his girlfriend lived. Invariably, he would fail to keep that excited preacher's voice down, and Claudia would groggily come out of her bedroom to join us in the living room for a nightcap. She never showed the slightest resentment for the invasion of her privacy. Claudia's understanding and tolerance is only a small part of the reason my friend Rob held a torch for her from high school on.

During my brief tenure in the music business, I was struck by how quickly my own tastes changed to accommodate hyper-commercial fare. The label was best known for its ability to break a song and create a hit. I had previously been a fan of several artists who were shopping for a deal. These included Mary McCaslin and John Hiatt. It was hard to take a pass on these great musicians, but our promotion and sales departments would not have been able to pave the way for their success. Even my fun, and very creative step cousin, Jody Uttal, who headed the label's publicity efforts, would likely not be a difference maker. These album oriented artists would be difficult to break into the top 40 singles charts. When I did uncover an artist of interest, other obstacles might arise. This was the case when I set up a showcase for TS Monk.

The leader of the band was the drummer son of the great jazz pianist, Thelonious Monk. I had met with the group a few times, heard their demo tape, and seen the band perform two live sets. I became excited about the Private Stock fit with this jazz-soul fusion group. Previously, the company had success with Cissy Houston, Whitney's mother and a member of the Sweet Inspirations. I pitched TS Monk as a possible extension of the label's proven capability in that genre.

On a Thursday afternoon at 3:30, the entire executive suite of the company gathered at Tramps, the site of the private showcase I had arranged. When I arrived fifteen minutes before my colleagues, I found an empty hall, with no one on stage or in the dressing room. TS Monk and his band hadn't yet arrived, and I was livid. I knew that once they did show up, they would need time to set up, which would take at least 30–45 minutes. And so, at 4 p.m. when I still hadn't heard from them, we all returned to the office. Larry let me know that he understood these things happen, but that he had no interest in me rescheduling the showcase. Any act that was looking for a deal but who couldn't make it to their own showcase was not ready for Private Stock.

While there were many good people pursuing a career in

music, I was becoming increasingly concerned about the quality of people I was meeting. Some were humorous caricatures. Juggie Gayles comes to mind. Juggie was a very short, mid-sixties promotion legend in the New York music scene. He would enter the office, sit down, then pop right back up, go to the door, and lock it. He would then turn to me and say "I got some really good shit. Want any?" Really? I thought. Would that be me at 65? I certainly hoped not.

I was beginning to lose perspective. Thinking I might emulate Peter Frampton's loosely curled mane, I got a perm. Unlike Frampton, my hair reacted by tightening up in a totally unattractive way. The perm "took" and left me with my hair way too close to my head, accentuating my nose. I looked absolutely rabbinic. For the next two months, I constantly worked on pulling out the kinks from my hair.

At about this time, Rob Blashek and his soon-to-be fiancé Carolyn were well into their Columbia Law School program. They graciously included me in a few evenings with their friends, which often featured Dan Castleman, who went on to become the number two behind Robert Morgenthau at the Manhattan District Attorney's office and appeared in several guest spots on *The Sopranos*. On another night, Rob and Carolyn invited me to join them and their friend Michelle, who was very attractive and sweet. I was told by Carolyn and Rob that she was interested in me. I never did anything about it, in part because I wasn't feeling terrific about myself. That was one that got away.

With the booming popularity of disco in the late seventies and early eighties, my job at Private Stock expanded to include promoting some of our acts to the big clubs in New York City. Every record label was remixing their product to conform to the taste of the dance party scene. Even my friend Elihu, who co-wrote a beautiful acoustic ballad called "Love Insurance," charted with a decidedly up-tempo version performed by Front Page and later, Sharon Redd. The scene was electrifying, but too decadent for me. I would get to know some of the top DJs at these clubs who had the ability to break a song by putting it into heavy rotation. My biggest success occurred when I had the top DJ at Studio 54 test-play our "Let's All Chant" by the Michael Zager Band. Once the dance floor filled, the song was replayed over ten times during the evening. It soon became a number one song on the *Billboard* Disco Chart and sold over five million copies.

Still, I was disheartened with this aspect of my job. The clubs and the DJs were generally populated by druggies and homosexuals who would aggressively hit on me. It wasn't easy being straight in those clubs. At the same time, Larry Uttal came out and hired his lover, Jim Massey, to oversee Private Stock's corporate marketing program. The couple's office behavior suggested to me that neither was keeping his eye on the company. Jim's aesthetically tasteful marketing campaign was splashy and expensive. Private Stock was the largest independent record label in the industry, but without the necessary managerial focus and a strong fiscal check on Jim's spending, the company wouldn't survive. In early 1979, Private Stock Records folded.

Chapter 6

Not Exactly Random

Private Stock's undoing was my opportunity to consider other career options—a do-over of sorts. RCA Records offered me a job in its A&R department, but I had soured on the music industry and many of the people who inhabited it. I still resisted the idea of going into a soulless bank training program. No, I wouldn't sell out just yet. I had long ago overcome my early learning issues and had become an avid reader of literary works and important nonfiction. I decided to speak with Bob Bernstein, our next-door neighbor in Scarsdale and co-owner of our family house on Martha's Vineyard. Bob was the head of Random House and appeared to be delighted to learn of my interest. His path to the top of the book industry was paved via the sales department. He urged me to consider taking the same route, and once I received a formal invitation to join Ballantine Books, the mass market and trade paperback division of Random House, I enthusiastically accepted.

I was to manage a sales territory that stretched from Eureka,

California, down to Carmel, where Clint Eastwood would become Mayor in a few years. I was responsible for a narrow, long slice of the northern California coastline that included most of San Francisco and some of the highest-volume retailers and wholesalers in the country. The job required me to move to San Francisco, and I did so just in time to attend the company's national sales conference, which happened to be held at the St. Francis Hotel.

As this was the pre-conference cocktail party and the eve of my first official day of work, I knew no one. We were a large group, and the room was jammed, particularly by the bar. I seemed invisible and felt the onus of introducing myself was on me. I started off a little tentatively. I had difficulty distinguishing between members of the sales team, various editors, and upper management. I noticed two of the service people out of uniform and dressed rather oddly. The very short man had a yellowed beard, a decrepit Van Dyke and he wore the thickest glasses I had ever seen. It came to me that they were dwarves or midgets (at the time, I couldn't quite recall the difference). Just as that thought raced through my brain, the woman looked up at me and introduced herself and her husband. They were not working for the hotel. Rather, they were Lester and Judy-Lynn del Rey, legends in the publishing business and the namesake of the most successful science fiction and fantasy imprint in publishing. Judy acquired and edited some of the biggest authors in fantasy and science fiction, from Philip K. Dick to her friend Isaac Asimov. I was surprised to learn that Judy-Lynn seemed to know everything about me—where I studied, my previous job in music, the kind of reputation I enjoyed, and so on. I wasn't sure what to make of her deep knowledge of my past and queried her on this.

Judy-Lynn explained that the Del Ray imprint derived over 40% of its entire volume from Northern California, so she and Lester made it a point to know the sales reps overseeing this most critical region. That meant she would spend a great amount of time getting to know me while continuing to keep tabs on my colleague Janis Donnaud, who was my counterpart responsible for sales within a similar and contiguous territory to the east. She worked with retailers in the East Bay, UC Berkeley, and Stacy's Books on Market Street. Given the high geographic concentration of Del Rey sales, Judy-Lynn was doing exactly what she should have been doing: guarding and growing the Del Rey franchise.

Before retiring for the night, Judy-Lynn let me know that I should consider creating two lists as soon as possible. For the first, I needed to identify my 25 top customers by sales volume. Easy peasy. The second list would contain 25 customers who could become part of the first list if handled correctly. Then she told me that in three weeks, there would be a private, invitation-only screening of a very special movie. On behalf of Ballantine Books' Del Rey imprint, Judy-Lynn had just acquired the movie's book tie-in rights, as well as book rights to any subsequent *Star Wars*-related films that might be released. She said she expected the movie to obliterate previous box office sales records—and that the tie-in book would follow suit.

I was given fifty guest tickets to the screening to distribute strategically. She had never felt so sure about the success of a project as she did this one. I took her at her word and ended up requesting, and receiving, an over-allotment, filling a total of 109 seats. At the end of the movie, the director, George Lucas, stood awkwardly looking at the entire audience on its feet clapping vigorously, while he tried to say a few words about his film. The result of this screening, and others throughout the country, was that *Star Wars* fever set in, and it was decided to ship the book earlier than planned. Well before the movie opened, the Del Rey book had sold five million copies. These were heady numbers, and they foretold a monster box office win. Del Rey made millions on the various books it published as tie-ins. Even the $75 *Art of Star Wars* coffee table book exceeded our expected sales by more than twofold.

Over the course of several regional and national meetings I got to know Janis Donnaud, my counterpart in Northern California. I believe Janis was from Tennessee, and she had a southern drawl that softened her very tough manner. She was feline in nature, guarded and inscrutable. Janis accentuated her perfectly oval face by wearing circular wire-rimmed glasses. Initially, I sensed some animosity from Janis, likely due to the way I got my job. Clearly, mine was a case of pure, unadulterated nepotism. I had waltzed my way into the company without any dues-paying experience. There was nothing I could do to alter her perception of me other than to put my head down and produce good work. As it happened, we shared a number of goals and identified some obstacles that were best dealt with together rather than apart.

Because the profile of the Northwestern reader differed so dramatically from those who came from other parts of the country, the views we might express to management were not often taken with the seriousness they deserved. For example, just as Northern California readers were very prone to read sci-fi and fantasy books, New Yorkers embraced romance titles. Whenever anyone from the New York home office came to meet with us, they told us we were underselling the midlist romance books. No matter that most of these books would ultimately be returned. The visiting NYC-based management team also seemed incapable of heeding our message to dress casually for sales calls, since none of my buyers expected—or even wanted—to see jackets and ties on publishing personnel who were calling on them. On these points, Janis and I agreed.

It would be some time before the next national conference, and in the interim, I cycled through my key clients at least five times, normally visiting them every other month. I had concluded that my accounts catered to a very literate, discerning customer base. This emboldened me to lean into books that I personally liked and could get behind. I articulated my excitement about these books and usually succeeded in advising buyers to think bigger numbers. I became focused on the power of merchandising, which allowed me to sell higher unit amounts. Most monthly lead titles could be ordered by the book or by the display unit. If a buyer felt that she should order, say, 15 copies of the lead title book, and the display unit came with 22 books, I would argue for taking on a display unit. This was especially true if the book's artwork was arresting and likely to contribute to its pull-through success. Cover art was a secret weapon of Judy-Lynn's, and it played a key role in breaking the *Dragonriders of Pern* trilogy, which led author Anne McCaffrey to become the first female winner of the Hugo award for science fiction.

I initiated a spirited debate during the next national sales conference, and Janis joined in support of my position. During the editors' sessions, we were informed that the *Stories of John Cheever* would be published in mass market paperback, and that the sales group would be provided materials to initiate the sell-in soon after the conference concluded. The hardcover version had enjoyed much success and was on the *New York Times* top 10 listing for many consecutive months. I knew this book would be a huge seller for my accounts. However, it seemed to me that the company was missing a wonderful opportunity to extend the life of the title.

Rather than go directly from hardcover to mass market, I argued that readers of John Cheever were likely to be fairly price-elastic and would be happy to pay the higher price of a quality trade-size paperback. Larry Kirshbaum, the CEO of the Random House-owned Warner Book Group, stood up and dismissively disagreed with me. WBG was the arm of the company that sold to rack jobbers, who in turn placed books in certain high traffic settings such as airports. Both Janis and I made the case that Larry's group would still get a bite at the apple, but we would be derelict if we did not first capitalize on the ongoing demand for the book. Especially given the length of the book, a trade paperback version was ideal, since it would improve the reading experience.

My suggestion was approved during the next day's session, and I felt very good about my modest contribution. When the *Stories of John Cheever* came out in trade format, it once again became a bestseller and remained near the top of the list for many months, after which the mass market version was published successfully.

I enjoyed my life in San Francisco. I had a terrific apartment on the fourth floor of a five-floor apartment building on Bay Street. I looked onto Fort Mason and, beyond that, the San Francisco Bay. Further, my bay window afforded me a view of the Golden Gate Bridge. I made friends but was struck by the general lack of authenticity I sensed from people who claimed to be my newest bestie. Discussions were generally kept on a surface level.

Ed O'Herron was a refreshing change from the insincerity I sensed in other San Franciscans. He lived in my building on the top floor directly above my apartment. Ed was forever entertaining notable leaders from San Francisco, Sacramento, and beyond. He was very close with Mayor Diane Feinstein and was part of the city's political and business fabric. Ed ran successful restaurants and bars in the Marina section of San Francisco as well as in and around the Bay Area. He had a broad pot belly and a nervous laugh. I assumed he was gay, but we never discussed the subject, and I never felt the need to know.

One evening, Ed suggested we go see Francis Ford Coppola's *Apocalypse Now*, which had just opened and was playing on Chestnut street. For over three hours, the movie depicted the relentlessly harrowing nature of the Vietnam War and soldiers' descent into a kind of hell, a terrible madness exacerbated by the evil that infected Colonel Kurtz, the character played by Marlon Brando. During the film, I couldn't help but be concerned for Ed, who had been deployed to Vietnam for three tours of duty in the early 1970s. Was he reliving an unspeakable period in his life? Did he have his own *Heart of Darkness* chapter? Should I offer to get up and leave the theater now, midway through? He whispered to me that he wanted to continue watching until the end, at which time we could go out for a drink and discuss the movie. At the film's conclusion, we filed out with the other moviegoers, who all appeared stunned by the film. Ed and I walked to Lombard Street and into His Majesty's Empire, a new English-styled pub he had wanted to try.

Once served our drinks, Ed gave me the green light to ask him anything. "Fire away" he said, and I told him I wanted to hear about his experience in Vietnam if it wasn't too difficult to talk about. He surprised me by breaking into a broad, mischievous grin. "My Vietnam War looked very different from what you and I just watched on screen," he said. He went on to explain that he was the senior officer of a four-man group whose job for the U.S. Army was to greet visiting entertainers and dignitaries, typically under the auspices of the USO, and to ensure that their in-country travel, dining, and safety needs were being met. If possible, the team's goal was to ensure that every visitor in its temporary care had a positive and meaningful experience while in Vietnam.

This was vintage Ed O'Herron. Only Ed could have summoned the luck of the Irish to land him the cushiest, most glamorous job in the Army. The array of notables he spent time with ranged from the legendary, thirty-year USO regular, Bob Hope, to the first-time tour for a *Playboy* Playmate of the Year. This was all of a piece: Ed's ability to entertain led to the job working for the Army and liaising with the USO. That job would lead to work for the City of San Francisco when Mayor Feinstein selected him to be the city's ambassador to the film industry. Finally, he was offered a very well-compensated position which required him to use the full array of his skills, growing rolodex, and unique experience to manage a multi-unit upscale dining restaurant group. He was very excited to apply his service philosophy across the five restaurants, two of which were in San Francisco and the other three in Palo Alto, Berkeley, and Mill Valley.

The most impactful relationship I had while in San Francisco was with Andrea Massey, a classmate from college.

During our Trinity days, I had known Andrea first as a high school friend—possibly girlfriend—of Jim Fairbrother, my freshman-year roommate. Andrea intrigued me. She had a wide circle of friends, but unlike so many others on campus, she tended to avoid crowds, preferring to have conversations that had depth and intimacy. Most of her good friends were artists, writers, musicians, dancers, and so on. Like Andrea, her friends were practitioners of various alternative mind-body health programs including tai chi, transcendental meditation, and yoga.

At first, I was not very attracted to her, notwithstanding evidence of her very alluring figure, which was difficult to assess due to her tomboyish sense of fashion. Andrea favored jeans and corduroy slacks and loose-fitting sweaters or sweatshirts. She had a bit of mystery to her. She used her sable-black, shoulder-length hair and her onyx eyes to communicate anger, happiness, love, confusion, or disappointment.

Andrea moved in with me on Bay Street, and although neither one of us would say the relationship was on our lists of top three all-time romances, we were more than happy to pass the time with each other. As Andrea became less guarded, my fondness for her intensified. She was principled and committed to living a productive life, even if the boundaries of that life were narrowly drawn. Andrea was highly spiritual, and her artistic output was an expression of that ethereal world view. She was playful, had a fantastic sense of humor, and a healthy sex drive. I tried to be ready with a joke and—forgive me—a schtup at all times.

Even with Andrea improving my outlook on life, I missed the East Coast. The dearth of family and the limited number of nearby good friends weighed on me. Andrea and I began to envision the two of us back east, and this became an attainable goal when Foote, Cone & Belding, the ad agency for which she worked, agreed to transfer Andrea to its NYC office. On the heels of Andrea's news, my management group at Ballantine Books offered to relocate me to New York or Connecticut. From there, I would be overseeing an important and very visible territory, which had been poorly managed by my predecessor.

Aside from "listening" to the wishes of a valued salesperson, the impetus for the offer was to introduce a new rep with fresh ideas to address the falloff in sales revenue from one of the company's largest customers. Caldor was a 145-store chain headquartered in Norwalk, Connecticut. Its volume potential was enormous, but you wouldn't know it from the mediocre numbers the account generated. I knew I would be judged by my success or failure with the chain. Could I create a turnaround—and if so, how would I accomplish this feat? My plan was simple because there were only a handful of ways to quickly juice sales.

The first thing I did was to postpone my upcoming relocation to New York City and ascertain whether my friend Elihu might want to share an apartment in Hartford. He did, and we quickly identified a new "cool" downtown development for brave urban hipsters. I felt that managing the Caldor account could not be done effectively from New York City. I had 125 customers, and one of them—Caldor—had 145 stores. All of those stores should be seen at least once a month, and every other month I aimed to complete a physical inventory. There weren't enough hours in the day for this schedule, and I would need to place some limitations on whom I saw monthly, quarterly, or annually. As I was creating my strategic plan, it became clear that I would need at least a year and a half to execute it and begin to see the fruits of its implementation. As to be expected,

Andrea and I amicably and mutually parted ways in a manner that implied a possible return to more intense days if and when I returned to New York City.

Buying for Caldor stores was centralized, and I believed that the buyer must have had some culpability for the poor showing of the Ballantine line of books. Indeed, on my first visit to Caldor's headquarters in Norwalk, I was thoroughly unimpressed with the book buyer, Paul Sammeth. Paul was in his early sixties and seemed to have no grasp on how to optimize the space allotted to the book department at each store. His systems were not at all reliable, which I proved with the results of each of the physical inventories I undertook throughout the chain. He hadn't a clue about merchandising. Over time, Paul loosened up and confided in me that he was planning to retire in about two years' time. He also began to let me write whatever I felt would increase sales for Caldor and, of course, my company. He had been impressed by positive feedback from the chain's in-field staff, who liked the attention I had given them. It was easy to differentiate the potential for sales between those books that would clearly be bestsellers and those that would die on the Caldor vine. I would order accordingly and would provide some balance by passing altogether on poorly matched titles. This was all a great success and, as a reward, I was invited into the home office to continue my career in publishing. Before the job they were considering for me opened up, I continued to do what I had done from my apartment (and the road) in Hartford.

John Fitzgerald, my friend and co-teacher at the summer school program for inner-city girls, had recently graduated from law school at the University of Connecticut. He and his classmates were an extremely welcoming group. They were argumentative, funny, and cultured. Through John, I became close friends with Peter Markle and his girlfriend Sue Silver. They were wonderful people—always there for me, and allowed me to traipse through their lives, sometimes wearing muddy galoshes. They made me feel as if I was the one person they were waiting for to make their world a more interesting, complete place. Peter had a professorial air about him, particularly when he was reading, biting down on his pipe and wearing his tweed, elbow-patched coat. He and I traded suggestions for films, books, and music. Peter worked in the district attorney's office in New Haven, and Susie was a case worker at Women in Crisis, a shelter for battered women and their children.

Another friend introduced to me via John Fitzgerald was David Gold. David reminded me of a young Billy Crystal and his girlfriend, a fiery Latina, was one of the world's biggest flirts.

During the time I was living in Hartford, I had the good fortune to be living with Elihu. His wide-ranging interests pointed him to an array of books and periodicals I might otherwise have missed. It was comforting to know that, in the event I was running late, Elihu could be the one thinking about dinner. Very often that meant a plate full of Matzo Brei or a brisket knish. Still, it beat McDonald's.

Then, about fourteen months later, as promised, I was transferred back into the New York office and was given one of the largest territories in the country. I also became another set of eyes and ears with respect to our competitors. I was thrown together with the promotion and design group, a three-person management team. Louis Martinez, Helen Griffin, Lee Northschield, and I would often go out for drinks after work.

I already knew them by way of their regular attendance at our sales conferences. One or more of them would be placed on the conference agenda and present to the group. During these friendly drinking sessions, the discussions would be substantive and occasionally turn critical of the publishing industry. Here were three members of senior management. If they were not happy with the state of publishing, I wondered, who was?

Chapter 7

Craig Fuller: What you wanna do?

My new roommate in New York was my old Trinity roommate, Tim Ghriskey. Tim was working for the ad agency Dancer Fitzgerald Sample. His key account was battery maker Duracell, a brand owned by PR Mallory Corporation, for whom he was the manager of media planning and buying. I liked the coincidence of Tim and my grandfather both working for PR Mallory, which was founded and controlled by my grandfather Jerry's client, Philip R. Mallory. Moving in with my old buddy made my transition back to New York easy.

By now, selling paperbacks and quality trade books was getting dull. I found it alarmingly easy to influence my clients, and I would need more challenges to hurdle if I was to stay engaged in publishing.

I had begun to neglect my lower-volume clients to have more time with the daughter of my parents' friends Jane and

Bob Peck. The two couples double dated and traveled together as twenty-somethings. Amy and I had known of each other for many years, chiefly through the boastful updates our moms would periodically provide each other. Amy was raised in Chappaqua, about 20 miles north of Scarsdale. I had only seen Amy twice—once as part of a large group attending the Moser family's annual holiday party, and then independently, surprising our mothers by each independently joining their luncheon. Well-bred, Amy told my mother that upon my return to New York, she would look forward to seeing me. She indicated that I should call her if I needed anything or wanted to meet for lunch or dinner. When my mother suggested I call Amy, I took down her contact coordinates and waited a few days before dialing her.

My recollection of Amy was very positive. She was bright, interesting, and beautiful. She had done very well at Middlebury and was selected to receive a prestigious Thomas J. Watson fellowship. Her fellowship project took her to the UK, where she researched the rise of female politicians in England at a time when Thatcher was just coming to power. She then travelled to Sweden, which was more progressive in its view of women in politics. Once the project was complete, Amy was offered a job assisting the political reporter, essayist, and talking head Richard Reeves. At that time, in 1980, Reeves was covering the presidential election and the rise of Ronald Reagan and writing a syndicated column for newspapers throughout the country. He was also working on a book retracing Alexis de Tocqueville's 1835 journey across America. Reeves wanted to explore de Tocqueville's concern that a democracy consisting of a majority of equals could abuse its power. The "tyranny of the majority" was no better than the unchecked power given to a single ruler, be it a monarch or a despot.

I got through to Amy as my mother urged, and she agreed to have dinner with me the following Friday. For some reason, I was so nervous about my upcoming date with Amy that Tim noticed and commented how unlike me it was to lose my cool before an innocuous first date—especially one that both she and I believed was being orchestrated by our parents for their amusement. Nevertheless, I couldn't deny the fact that my breath had quickened, and my mouth became dryer as Friday night drew nearer. I found myself softly singing "Amie" as if I were Craig Fuller, the song's writer and lead singer of Pure Prairie League.

I had planned a full evening. First, I stopped by Amy's apartment on Broadway and 8th Street east of Fifth Avenue in the Village. Her roommate, Terri Byrne, was away for the weekend, so Amy invited me up for a glass of wine and some cheese and crackers. I was floored when she opened the door to let me in. She was wearing a very sexy, ecru-colored, Stevie Nicks-styled outfit, notable for its sheer, flowy material and fringed shawl. On her feet she wore light sand-colored boots that had laces crossing up her legs. I was smitten at once. I took a deep breath and told her we needed to get going if we were going to make our dinner reservation in time.

I had chosen a fun, interesting place rather than trying too hard to impress by selecting a "fine" dining establishment. We grabbed a cab and I directed the driver to 37th and 10th Avenue, which was then a desolate part of Manhattan. We walked into Guido's Macaroni Factory, whose front room was filled with pasta molds, pasta boxes, and large vats, with flour spills all over the floor. The back room was obscured by beaded drapes and an old woman with significant facial hair, who was either the welcoming committee or standing guard. With a nod to the woman, we entered the back room. I had been to Guido's a number of times and explained to Amy that it was a music industry haunt. The restaurant made its own wine, and oddly, there did not seem to be a difference in taste or temperature between the red and the white wine. Billy Joel was a regular at Guido's, and his song "A Bottle of Red, A Bottle of White" was written with Guido's in mind. The restaurant was a convivial place, with diners getting to know one another under the gaze of Grandma, the hirsute old lady who could only speak Italian.

Then we were off again, this time to the Ritz, a club and music venue on 13th Street, two blocks east of Fifth Avenue. One of the benefits of leaving the music business was that it freed me from having to consider commercial potential and helped me return to an earlier time, when listening to new music was fulfilling and absorbing. I may have been gone from the music business, but I was not forgotten. My friend and former boss at Private Stock, Steve Scharf, had played me an advance copy of the debut album from a new Irish band. The album, *Boy*, produced by the great Steve Lillywhite, featured the infectious single "I Will Follow" and was to be supported by a tour. U2's first show ever performed in the U.S. was the concert Amy and I were bound for.

The Ritz was quiet when we arrived. There were no more than 100 to 125 people milling around waiting for the music to begin, so we were able to stand right up front next to the stage. Notwithstanding the poor turnout, Bono, the Edge, and bandmates Adam Clayton and Larry Mullen did not disappoint. The ever-energetic Bono was particularly animated during the show, and the vibrant musical shadings—with the bright, sparkly percussive sound—as well as my proximity to Amy, made for a memorable show.

Once the concert was over, I suggested we go to the nearby Cedar Tavern on University for a drink. Although it was getting late, Amy agreed to join me for a nightcap. Amy was wonderful company. Easy to talk to, she seemed so interested in what I had to say. I am not sure how long we talked, but I think we closed down the Tavern. After doing so, I walked Amy back to her apartment on 8th Street. This had been a perfect night, and I was not going to mar it by potentially misreading Amy's interest in me. So, once we were in her lobby, I told her what a great time I had and that we should definitely do it again. She agreed and gave me a kiss, the meaning of which was not clear to me. I made it back to my apartment at around 2 a.m. So many thoughts raced through my mind, and I had trouble getting to sleep. I knew one thing: although I had promised myself I would wait until I was 35 to get married, I was going to break that vow and propose to Amy well before then.

The next day I was unable to think straight. Tim was amused by how flummoxed I was. I hadn't yet heard from Amy, and it had been about a week since our date. Careful not to appear too interested, I went out to meet my friend Steve, his new girlfriend, and her friend Evelyn. We met up at Mikell's, a favorite club of mine on the Upper West Side, where for several years the jazz fusion funk band Stuff was the house band. Stuff was a loose amalgamation of extremely talented session musicians. The great drummer, Bernard Purdie provided persistent and infectious grooves accentuated by ghosted half note syncopation. In an embarrassment of riches, Steve Gadd also played with the band.

Gadd, who was responsible for the dynamic, breathtaking drum solo on Steely Dan's *Aja*; Cornell Dupree and Eric Gale on guitar; Richard Tee on keyboards; and Bernard Edwards on bass guitar. The music was so good, it succeeded in keeping my mind from wandering back to Amy.

I finally reached out to Amy by phone. On several occasions I tried her but without any luck. I had left a cool, noncommittal message on her voice mailbox. This not hearing, not knowing, was not easy, and I called her several more times, always hanging up before being faced with the bell tone instructing me to leave a message. My mood darkened. Then on Monday afternoon, I received a postcard depicting hundreds of pastel-colored tulips. It read:

> "Dear Ralph: I am in California on business and wanted to thank you for the wonderful night last Friday. I had the time of my life. I really look forward to our next rendezvous. Be back this Tuesday. Amy"

I didn't want to read too much into the text of the card, but my mood swung to the happy side of the spectrum. Could Amy really be interested in me? *Me*???

I called Amy later the next day and asked her out for Friday night. She said "Absolutely!" with a verve that suggested that she, too, was looking forward to our next evening together. At that time, most non-Asian Americans still considered sushi to be a fringe cuisine that had potential health risks. Once we tried sushi, we loved it. Amy and I began frequenting a Japanese sushi restaurant a few blocks from her apartment. As on our first date, I was overflowing with talk, and I felt Amy holding on to the threads of my stories for dear life.

On one of our evenings together she was in my bedroom and opened the closet. "What's this," she asked when confronted by a woman's robe. This led to a frank discussion about Evelyn—the friend of Steve's girlfriend with whom I had been paired at Mikells—and our post-Mikell's activity. In response, Amy confessed that after our first date, while in California, she had a "late night" fueled by liquor, Champagne, and jet lag. Yes, *late night* meant that she had ended up with Leonard, an older West Coast-based colleague who was no doubt quite pleased with himself. When I considered her evening with Leonard and mine with Evelyn, it occurred to me that we both needed to get something out of our system as we prepared to take on a long-term, monogamous relationship.

Amy and I settled into an increasingly comfortable rhythm. She did surprise me one Sunday afternoon as we were returning from visiting her parents in Chappaqua. Amy and I were driving on the Hutchinson Parkway when I looked over and noticed she was quietly crying. I asked her what was wrong and she wouldn't say. I pulled off at the southbound Mamaroneck Avenue exit and parked the car at the Weinberg Sanctuary, which was only 75 yards from the parkway ramp. After several attempts to discover what was wrong and to determine if I had done anything to bring on her tears, Amy told me that it was just the Sunday weepies, an affliction that ran in her family but made no sense to me. Amy said she was dreading our plans that evening with our friends Jim Fairbrother and Jenny Doctorow. The weepies had set in, and there was no way to chase them away. This was the first time I had encountered the Peck family proclivity to form their own very tight circle and, from time to time, to avoid outsiders. I was on notice to treat her with kid gloves during her bouts of introversion.

Despite Amy's trepidation to go out with Jim and Jenny that Sunday night, they were our go-to couple for intellectual exploration and cultural pursuits. Jim was my freshman roommate and, although he transferred to Wesleyan, a school that better suited him, we stayed in close contact. His father died at the age of 40, a victim of a massive heart attack. Jim believed his time would be similarly truncated, and sadly that proved to be the case.

Jenny was the older daughter of Edgar (E.L.) Doctorow and Helen Setzer. On Jim and Jenny's suggestion, the four of us rented a house together in Sag Harbor, just a five-minute drive from Jenny's parents' summer home. On one or two occasions, Edgar made sure to include Jim and me in the weekly Saturday softball game held in Mashashimuet Park. This game was originally arranged by Ken Auletta, the biographer, media critic, and political commentator. On any given weekend, the lineups might feature a host of A- and B-listers from the literary and media worlds including Edgar, Ken, Peter Matthiessen, Kurt Vonnegut, George Plimpton, Lori Singer, Tom Wolfe, and others.

I had been following the global rise of electronic publishing and was very excited about being part of the shifting technology that, I believed, was likely to alter and disrupt the publishing business. This I took on faith. I could point to a flurry of activity as large data providers—from AT&T and IBM to CBS and Chemical Bank—entered the field. I urged Random House's management to seek a leadership role in the e-publishing field on the ground floor and enjoy its first-mover advantage over other publishers. But no one "heard" me. Where were the visionaries to lead us into the 21st century? Certainly not at Random House. I concluded that I needed to join a forward-leaning company whose vision aligned with mine. Never mind that if Random House had listened to me, they could easily have lost all their investment, as it was way too early to step into these untested waters.

I reached out to Keith Benzel, a soft-spoken, self-assured friend of Jim Fairbrother's who had made his way to the once cutting-edge companies AOL and Prodigy. Within a few years, Keith had been promoted several times and was well situated to give me some sense of the opportunity ahead. He, too, expressed optimism for the business potential of its application in technology, particularly with respect to certain vertical markets like publishing where the fit was clearly there. The addressable market for electronic publishing was thought to be vast. He suggested I marry my publishing experience with a business degree and make myself an in-demand candidate for the field. As I thought about it, this advice made a lot of sense. Amy was supportive of my decision to explore an MBA program, as was my father, who suggested I contact his own mentor, Monty Shapiro.

To all who knew him, my father, Warren, was extremely serious and impressive. A lawyer-turned-businessman-turned-pro-bono difference-maker, he was a precocious child who tested boundaries. Dad was innately smart and entered college at the age of fifteen. My father's memoir, the aptly titled *Man in Motion*, provides a full account of his career, the highlights of which include his partnership stints at several law firms, his election to the New York State Assembly, his rise to the vice chairmanship of Plessey—a large British-based multinational that, at its peak, employed over 80,000 people—and, later, upon his so-called retirement, the founding of a nonprofit law firm for children's rights in New York City. Dad was smart enough to win either side of any argument and had an unerring sense of right and wrong. Whenever I did something stupid that ran counter to his moral compass, he would let me know. Invariably, no punishment was as much of a deterrent as was his disappointment in me.

Back to my father's mentor... Shapiro was a gruff, no-nonsense businessman who sat on the Plessey board. He had been Chairman of General Instrument but was retired by the time I met him. General Instrument was predominantly a semiconductor and electronics manufacturer that made parts for televisions and cable set-tops. Monty had led General Instrument into a series of difficult acquisitions that required significant negotiating skill, which he had in spades. His colorful dressing-down of those colleagues who had failed him was legendary. He did not suffer fools gladly, which, of course, gave me reason to be nervous when I sat down across from him in his office.

Monty was an adjunct professor at NYU's Stern School of Business, which was why my father had me reach out to him. Monty had only one question for me: "what would you do with an MBA?" I responded with a quip: "I would display my degree certificate on one of the walls of my office." My response was apparently good enough to earn Monty's praise of me to my father and generated a critically important recommendation on my behalf to the Stern School's dean of admissions.

I heard from NYU six weeks later. I had been accepted to the Stern School of Business Management and was invited to join the school's incoming class of 1982, which would matriculate that September, 1980. I contacted my boss at Ballantine and let him know that I was giving him notice of my resignation. In my mind, I had already begun to leave. I pictured myself as one of Del Rey's sci fi characters who gradually loses corporeality and becomes dust over time. This state of being negatively affected the quality of my work during my last few months at the company. It also led to a flagging of my attention to the details that had heretofore enabled me to individualize my working relationship with my accounts. I had a tinge of guilt regarding the imperfect shape in which I was leaving my buyers. This in turn, would make it difficult on my successor.

Still, I was now looking ahead. I was worried about my math skills and wondered if I was numerate enough to handle some of the coursework. I cursed my silly, snooty attitude toward my college classmates who by now had several years of experience in bank training programs, while I had been wasting time in the arts (though, actually, I never considered any of my endeavors to be a waste of time). So, in advance of returning to school, I took an intensive calculus class, which was the best thing I ever did. My fear of math melted away, and the mystery of its applications to real-life problems was suddenly made clear.

NYU Stern had no traditional campus. Rather, its classrooms, computer labs, administrative offices, and dining facilities were housed in two innocuous buildings near Wall Street. It was a far cry from the gracious, ivied buildings of the University of Virginia, where my old roommate, Tim Ghriskey, was working on his master's in business administration. Tim had resigned from DFS, the ad agency, about the same time that I informed Random House of my decision to resign. The timing was perfect, since Amy had decided to invite me to move in with her, following her roommate Terri's pending move to Chicago. Neither Tim nor I would need to replace the other with someone new.

The absence of a traditional campus made for a more work-like, 9-to-5 experience. Nevertheless, I was able to connect with several of my classmates, some of whom would be part of my team for projects that required us to work in groups. My male classmates were almost uniformly focused on obtaining investment banking careers, and so I was in the minority as I envisioned myself working at a high-level, marketing-driven company like Procter & Gamble. One of our team projects involved game theory and the management of a fictional company called Praxis, an industrial materials company. We were pitted against three other fictional companies in the same field. Every day for many weeks, we were required to input our responses to changes in the market as well as the moves of our competitors. Every night, the mainframe computer would digest all the information from the four teams and deliver the current state of play the next morning. As in real life, how we optimized scarce resources would be the key to distinguishing ourselves. Would we opt for a push or a pull marketing strategy? How much of any free cash flow should be allocated to R&D?

My Praxis group included three of my NYU friends: Ruth Zielan, Diane Krantz, and Bob Leanard. Ruth was an interesting, hard-to-read woman. She had cool cobalt eyes that seemed to have greater depth than normal. Her skin was almost translucent, giving her a fairy-like quality. Ruth often came at things from a different angle that illuminated an important issue that had not yet been uncovered by the group. She was engaged to the son of the founder-owner of the Subway sandwich chain, and after NYU, Ruth would go into commercial real estate with LaSalle in Chicago.

Bob Leanard was from Long Island. He was single-minded in his pursuit of his degree and, he hoped, a job with Merrill Lynch's capital markets desk. He spent all his free time following the stock ticker located in the school's dining hall. He did know his hockey, and this was an era when both the Rangers and the Islanders were more than competitive. Starting in 1979, the Islanders would win four consecutive Stanley Cups. Our classmates followed the progress of our local hockey teams very closely.

Diane Krantz was my favorite classmate at NYU. She had a wonderful combination of intellect, social awareness, and humor. Our interchanges were always deeply satisfying. She was friends with Billy Bernstein, Bob and Helen's youngest of their three boys. Her understanding of global events and their impact on the U.S. economy and U.S. companies was well beyond that of any other classmates of mine. Her humor could be sly and on point. When the group completed the game theory group project, she suggested we add a tagline to our cover page: "Remember: Praxis Makes Perfect."

I'm not sure whether I would have applied to business school were it not for Amy. She gave me a reason to better myself and my future. Our parents were not oblivious to the seriousness of our relationship and, at least on my side, my mother and father seemed to encourage it. Both Bob Peck, Amy's dad, and my dad, Warren, flew planes for the fun of it. When my father heard Amy and me discussing the possibility of driving thirteen hours to Nova Scotia for a five-day vacation, he offered to fly us in his plane. Given the length of the flight, he asked Jim Cornell, his friend and professional pilot, to join him as co-pilot. Amy and I were dropped off at Halifax Airport. From there, we rented a small green Peugeot sedan and drove the seventy-five minutes to our unassuming bed and breakfast called Milford House. Guests at Milford House could stay in the main house or in individual cabins, all of which were situated near the edge of two large, connected lakes. When we checked in, I indicated that we were on our honeymoon. As a result, we were given the most private cabin, and guests would nod to us knowingly at meals. For several days, we paddled canoes and explored the banks of the lakes. We would pull into an inlet, then stop to read aloud to each other from *The Phantom Tollbooth*, a favorite of Amy's.

We talked about our friends, family, and goals. What would make a life well-lived? For Amy, it was to be the matriarch of a close-knit family and to make a meaningful contribution to help improve the lives of less fortunate people. I said a well-lived life would be to provide for my family and to grow into a less selfish, more worldly person. We were *simpatico*. The only lingering issue was how we would bridge our opposing views vis-à-vis the relative merits of being socially involved extroverts or introverts who always put family first. I agreed with Amy's family-first approach but worried that its logical extension would lead to a form of inbreeding. Where would the engine of personal growth come from if not in the vastness of the world and its variety of people? Foregoing the potential for our own growth by severely limiting the time we spend with others would be a disservice to children, who would not have been privy to a healthy dose of parental modeling. I made the point that I was absolutely all for family-first—as long as it didn't lead to family-only.

Upon our return to New York, I became convinced that

Amy and I should get married as soon as practical. I told my parents that I was likely to propose soon. My mother offered me her engagement ring, which I gratefully accepted. I also spoke with Amy's dad to get his OK before I popped the question. Amy and I were fans of an Upper East Side restaurant called Vivolo, which inhabited two floors of a brownstone on East 74th Street between Fifth and Madison Avenues. I decided it would be the perfect backdrop for my proposal.

Unfortunately, when I told Amy that we were going to one of our favorite restaurants, she said she wasn't in the mood and didn't want to change into more Vivolo-appropriate clothes. When it was clear I wasn't going to convince her to change her mind, I said, "Fine, meet me at Route 55," a hamburger joint on the south side of West 72nd Street. "From there we can walk a few blocks to Trax," a music club close to Route 55. Although I had brought the engagement ring with me, I was still simmering at her obstinacy when Amy showed up. I decided to wait until I was in a better frame of mind before asking her to marry me.

Amy was not at her best. She spent the better part of twenty minutes complaining about something or somebody. I had tuned out. It wasn't until we arrived at Trax that she became her more upbeat, happy self. Trax had a double bill of two very loud punk bands, The Dead Kennedys and the Sick F*cks. It no longer mattered to me whether my proposal was done romantically or not—I just needed to have it done. So, despite the ear-splitting music, I yelled out my proposal to Amy. She could not hear me, and so I pulled out the heirloom diamond ring. When one of Trax's revolving spotlights landed on the diamond, Amy caught the sparkle of the diamond and understood what I was asking.

She said yes, and I couldn't have been happier. Then, later in the evening, as I was preparing for bed, I found Amy softly crying. She claimed that these were happy tears, but I wasn't sure she was being totally truthful with me.

The planning and preparations for the wedding were underway. To avoid unnecessary conflicts, I promised myself that I would agree with everything Amy said or suggested. No need to get her hackles up, particularly since Amy had an aesthetic that I trusted fully. Amy's parents' house in Chappaqua was the site of our low-key and joyous wedding. Amy had worked for Abigail Kisch, thought to be the best caterer in the New York tri-state area. Her old employer had become too fancy and rigid for what we had in mind for our wedding. Amy's mom, Jane, fell hard for two creative and vibrant young restaurateurs from the Greenwich Village restaurant Il Cantinori, Rob and Sylvan, who created beautiful, abundant displays using food as a brightly colored design element for special occasions. Il Cantinori provided us with outstanding Italian food, which was served on mustard-colored plates. Given the limited seating and table space, many of us needed to carefully balance our meals on our thighs. The photographer we engaged had a fondness for snapping pics of our guests' haphazardly arranged feet.

Amy and Jane had envisioned a bright, sunny day in mid-June, where some of our guests could be seated outside on her parents' wraparound porch overlooking a lake. Flowers were strewn everywhere, including on the pathway to the dock. Jane had arranged for Richard Eudice, her partner in her floral business, to row to the middle of the lake and release helium balloons to celebrate our union. Music, in the form of a hammered dulcimer, was provided by Bill Peak, the boyfriend of my friend and former roommate Claudia Steinberg. Other than Bill, I was the only one in the house—including Amy—who knew our wedding song, "The Dutchman." Written by Michael Smith and performed flawlessly on vinyl by Steve Goodman, "The Dutchman" tells the tale of an old man entering his second childhood and being lovingly cared for by his wife of many decades. Here are a few of the stanzas from the song's lyrics:

> *The Dutchman's not the kind of man*
> *Who keeps his thumb jammed in the dam*
> *That holds his dreams in,*
> *But that's a secret only Margaret knows.*
>
> *When Amsterdam is golden in the summer,*
> *Margaret brings him breakfast,*
> *She believes him*
> *He thinks the tulips bloom beneath the snow*
>
> *Let us go to the banks of the ocean*
> *Where the walls rise above the Zuiderzee.*
> *Long ago, I used to be a young man*
> *And dear Margaret remembers that for me.*
>
> *The Dutchman still wears wooden shoes,*
> *His cap and coat are patched with the love*
> *That Margaret sewed there,*
> *Sometimes he thinks he's still in Rotterdam.*

And he watches the tug-boats down canals
And calls out to them when he thinks he knows
 the Captain.
Till Margaret comes to take him home again.

Through unforgiving streets that trip him,
 though she holds his arm.
Sometimes he thinks he's alone and he calls her name.

And he sees her for a moment, calls her name,
She makes the bed up singing some old love song,
A song Margaret learned when it was very new.
He hums a line or two, they sing together in the dark.
The Dutchman falls asleep and Margaret blows the
 candle out.

Despite the *Farmer's Almanac* and Jane and Amy's best wishes, our wedding day wasn't bright and sunny. Not even close. Rather, the weather was raw and stormy, with torrential rain that never let up. At least we needn't angst over what we should do—it was clear that the storm would hover over us for the duration of the wedding. The crowd and the rain gave new meaning to the word "overflow." The weather precluded any outdoor seating, which taxed the limited arrangements we could provide indoors. The large, framed windows overlooking the pond were completely steamed up, obscuring the view of Richard's valiant efforts to row on the now-rising lake. No matter—our guests were grinning from ear to ear and were just as attentive during Rob Blashek's best man roast of me as they were during Rabbi Jack Stern's pronouncement that we were now man and wife.

It seemed to Amy and me that the day had just begun, but we were already saying the last of our goodbyes. We had a room at the Rye Town Hilton and tickets to London for the next day. I was looking forward to connecting with my new bride, but when we unpacked at the hotel, Amy realized she had left one of her bags at her parents' house. Moreover, Amy was anxious to chat with her parents and sisters to dish and to get their unvarnished reaction to the wedding. She took my car, and while she was having a great time with her family, I called up my younger brother Michael, who met me in the lobby of the hotel where we watched a Yankees game and chatted over a beer.

For our honeymoon, Amy and I traveled to England's southern coastline after first spending a few days in London. While in the capital city, we stayed at the legendary, elegant but understated Connaught Hotel. We would return to this bastion of incomparable, old-line service in September of the following year. At that time, immediately following our check-in, there was a rap on the door. I opened it, and there stood the valet, who wanted to know what he could do to make our stay more comfortable. When I told him we appreciated his offer but that we were in no need of his services, he smiled and said, "Very well, sir." But before pivoting away from our door, he added, "I believe these are yours, sir," and presented me with a small silver tray upon which rested my missing gold button cufflinks and a pair of my underwear, which had been newly laundered, stiffly ironed, folded, and placed in its own plastic wrapper. When it became clear that I had left these items behind during our honeymoon stay a year earlier, I was amazed. "Why didn't you just send these back to me instead of having to store them for so long," I asked. "What if I never returned?" "Oh, sir," he replied, "our guests always return."

Before heading south on our honeymoon, we had a memorable evening at Annabel's, a private club known for its fine dining and tables filled with elegant, older, well-heeled gentlemen and their much younger, bejeweled female companions. Amy and I also attended the musical *Cats*, which wouldn't open on Broadway for another five months. Does it make me petty to enjoy arts-related programs more when I see them well in advance of the great unwashed? Think *Hamilton* in its initial run at the Public Theater or, yes, U2 in 1980 at a nearly empty club.

On our way driving to Land's End and Penzance, we stopped at Stourhead, said to be "to gardens, what Mozart is to music." It did not disappoint. Part of the National Trust, this vast garden boasts well-orchestrated shrubbery and flowers. The gardens are so vast that within them lies a small village with three small shops and a magnificent church. The lawns and trees were scrupulously clipped.

When we got to Chideock in Dorset, we pulled the car into a perfectly charming thatched-roof inn called The Chimneys. The inn had just four guest rooms. Ours was immaculately clean and featured brightly colorful rose-patterned wallpaper, rugs, a bedspread, and—oh yes—bouquets of freshly picked roses.

We awoke to a beautiful day and, after breakfast, walked to Golden Camp, one of the highest peaks in the area. Although the hillside was quite steep, the climb was made easier by the crystalline clarity of the azure sky and the unfettered views up and down the English coast. It was exhilarating. By early afternoon, we had returned to The Chimneys, showered, and changed out of our hiking clothes into something more presentable. Clouds began to appear, and the wind picked up. It wasn't stormy—at least not yet. Taking our cue from Mother

Nature, we drove the four miles to Lyme Regis, a quintessential British beach town, with its winding streets, pastel houses, and boardwalk connecting the main town with the beach. We decided to walk the full length of the long jetty, where Meryl Streep was memorably filmed in her cowled cape in Harold Pinter's recent film adaptation of John Fowles' novel, *The French Lieutenant's Woman*.

We left The Chimneys the next morning and headed southwest to Tintagel Castle in Northern Cornwall. The castle, a medieval fortification, is said to have been the conception site of King Arthur. After our close inspection of the ruins and the castle structure itself, we were off to Port Gaverne and its companion fishing village, Port Isaac.

When we got to Port Gaverne, we checked in and headed to a nearby cliff path that took us up above the village and out to the water. It was a bright, sunny day, and the view of the town's stone and whitewashed houses, the undulating green hills rolling towards the cliffs that dropped hundreds of feet to the town's rocky beach, was spectacular. And of course, there was the majestic, rolling Atlantic Ocean.

Our new accommodations were in a 15th-century inn, nestled within a deep hillside cleft. I continued my evening habit of letting Amy dress for dinner without me, while I went downstairs to the bar area. There I befriended other guests—all older than me—who had gathered for drinks. I loved these fellow travelers and the ease with which I engaged them. Throughout our travels, I became acquainted with many interesting people who made up a series of pre-dinner groups. I would often join them for a cigarette on the sly, since Amy believed I had quit the nasty habit. I went through more mints and gum on that trip than I care to remember. There was also something very sexy about waiting for my new bride to join me and meet my new circle of friends, especially since Amy always managed to look fetching at dinner.

The following morning, we motored to Dartington, where we spent some time at the Cider Press, a crafts enclave that lived up to its reputation for high-quality goods. However, it wasn't until we reached Bath and headed to Pulteney Bridge that we found a truly unique—and, to our sensibility, stunning—retailer. The store was called Coexistence. Its concept was to display an expertly curated set of antiques interspersed with design-forward modern home goods, fabrics, furniture, and furnishings. The wide array of patterns and textures strewn around the store somehow worked. The store even offered customers weekly classes on interior design. We took the owner's card in the event we were struck with the need to become the store's New York City franchisee. Amy had her eye on a few items, but they were very expensive and would require even more to safely ship home. Just as we were leaving, I spied a small but weighty wooden bowl circa 1720. We bought the bowl, and today, over forty years later, we keep it filled with colorful marbles. The bowl is a physical touchstone to the very start of our married lives.

Chapter 8

Going Downtown

During my second year at NYU Stern, my schedule had to accommodate the internship I had been offered by American Express. Fortunately, Amex was headquartered only a short walk south of the NYU Stern program's two buildings in the Wall Street area. At the time—in the early 1980s—Amex was considered among the very best financial services marketers in the world. Its products and services commanded higher prices than those of other card companies, even as its revenue growth outpaced competitors. It could do so because of the wide gap between the perceived value of its offerings—which is subjective—and their "real" value, derived from their actual utility. The positive spread between real and perceived value was due to the company's industry-leading marketing and operational prowess.

Functionally, Amex cards were no different from Diners Club or bank cards like Visa and Mastercard. But the fee differential was significant, and self-perpetuating. The improved margins and greater free cash flow funded new marketing programs designed to make the intangible benefits of card membership feel more concrete. Examples included the ability to replace any lost or stolen card within 24 hours, which required significant operational sophistication, and exclusive access to purchase premium tickets for sporting and cultural events before they sold out.

For service establishments (SEs), Amex offered invaluable data about their customer base. This might include how many customers lived within a 10-mile radius, how many were from out of state, and how active those cardmembers were in their spending patterns. For example, this data set could help a retailer optimize media purchases by targeting its core customer—whether hyper-local or regionally distributed.

My internship was within American Express's Travel Related Services group, known by its acronym, TRS. The three core groups that made up TRS in the early 1980s were the Travel Agencies (including specialized payment systems such as travelers checks), Service Establishment, and Card Marketing. Service Establishment marketing was organized by industry. For the internship, I was placed in the Airlines group, which was headed by Cathy Cronway. My project—my deliverable—was a study on the airline industry in which I was to identify an optimal pricing structure and surface any opportunities to enhance the contribution to or from Amex's airline industry partners.

The airlines were critically important to Amex, given the size of their charge volume and their high visibility within the travel industry. Over the course of many months, I became acquainted with the company's fee price sensitivity analysis as well as a competitor fare study. Bridging the two reports was difficult, since it was unknowable how much of Amex's SE fees would be passed on to the air travelers versus absorbed as a margin dampener. While still finishing my MBA, I completed the study. To much fanfare, I was asked to present my findings and suggested next steps to senior management, including John Sutvan, the Senior Executive Vice President in charge of all TRS. Sutvan asked a few somewhat challenging questions, which I easily answered. While I cannot recall the details of my findings, the key takeaway is that I "passed" the internship with flying colors.

As a result, almost immediately following my presentation, I was offered a full-time position to commence at the end of the summer, after my graduation from NYU Stern. I was pleased but wanted to see what else I might be able to find within the company. SE marketing was fine, but not nearly as interesting as Card Marketing, with its multitude of strategic levers at its disposal.

While I went through the motions of interviewing with other consumer brand marketing companies, I was a self-proclaimed New York City snob and not particularly interested in leaving the city for some Midwestern alternative. That ruled out Procter & Gamble, Kellogg's, and countless others. I did consider companies in reverse-commutable proximity to the city. These included Purchase, New York-based PepsiCo and Wilton, Connecticut-based Richardson-Vicks, whose sensitivity to its neighbors and embrace of modern architecture were evident in the siting of its headquarters—tucked into a densely forested area, the trees protected it from overwhelming the site lines of its neighbors. Still, did I really want to reverse-commute every day to put my imprimatur on DayQuil or Vicks VapoRub?

What I most wanted was to be part of the Card Marketing group, which was led by Diane Sheib, an impressive woman who had advanced up the organization quickly. After I interviewed for a spot on the team, Diane arranged for me to meet with one of her directors, Brian Kleinberg. Brian was an unassuming, plainspoken man who was very smart and generally underestimated. We got along very well, and he reported back to Diane that he would like to have me in his group. Diane made me an offer to become manager of Gold Card marketing, reporting to Brian, and she also let me know that I would be part of the company's Executive Development Program (EDP).

The purpose of the EDP was to fast-track certain employees which the company believed exhibited promise and give them as much visibility into the company's workings as possible. We met monthly, and on any given month we might hear from Lou Gerstner, the CEO of TRS (and later IBM) and President of Amex's parent company. Or Jerry Welsh, American Express's Executive Vice President of Worldwide Marketing and Communications, might present to the EDP. Jerry was responsible for undertaking what may have been the first modern national cause marketing campaign. By all accounts, it was a very big success. American Express donated a very small piece of every transaction (one penny each) to the Statue of Liberty Foundation, which needed funds for its long-overdue renovation. In aggregate, the pennies added up to approximately two million dollars—but the impact of this relatively modest donation was said to be equivalent to twenty million dollars of advertising. We measured awareness of the campaign among cardholders and prospective cardholders and found that Amex had successfully established its charitable link to Lady Liberty.

American Express was a market-leading, innovative company, and as a new employee, I felt proud to be on the inside. At the time, American Express was the largest non-governmental mailer in the United States. The Gold Card marketing program relied heavily on direct response mail and generally eschewed other media. Unlike the Green Card, the Gold Card was a partnership with banks: Amex would provide marketing, white-glove servicing, and operational excellence, while the banks brought their credit lending expertise.

Direct response programs had several benefits for us. We controlled the components of each mailing and used sophisticated tools to track and analyze results. In a typical million-piece mailing, we pre-selected test cells of statistical relevance, each containing 5,000 to 15,000 discrete addresses. The prospective cardmembers in these test cells received a slightly different version of the core mailing package. When we measured response rates, we could easily determine whether to incorporate that change in the next wave of mailings.

I wanted to test the impact of utilizing a shiny gold hot stamp on the upper-left face of the envelope, as well as a new mailing "legacy" brochure. With the aid of Amex's corporate historian and a trove of evocative, sepia-tinted photographs, I developed a new eight-page brochure that celebrated the company's mid-19th-century past, including its involvement with the Pony Express and Wells Fargo. The results of both the brochure mailing and gold hot stamp test cells were overwhelmingly positive. The core mailing yielded a solid 2.6% return rate, while the hot stamp and legacy brochure test cells boosted the response to an unheard-of 4.0% and 4.2%, respectively. These were very significant results, and I would go on to test other creative elements, including using personalized versus generic salutations in the solicitation letters. I also ran the Green-to-Gold Card conversion program.

Following these results, Brian asked me to run the more dynamic student card marketing program, where I would oversee several managers and have leeway to try approaches beyond direct mail. The backbone of the student card marketing program was the on-campus network of "Take One" student ambassadors. In exchange for placing and maintaining Take One applications at their schools, these students were paid a small portion of their schoolmates' first year Amex membership fees.

The student market was very different from the Gold Card market. Students were looking for utility and a way to feel accepted. Gold Card members were embracing the *status* of the Gold Card, particularly before the Platinum Card was introduced in late 1984. Notwithstanding the fact that our research found student cardholders to be less likely to default than the average cardmember, prospective student cardmembers were concerned about rejection. To address this, I came up with a few means of signaling that American Express "got them" and warmly welcomed them into its club.

I felt that the Campus Ambassadors were being underutilized. In coordination with this "boots on the ground" group, we launched a series of sponsorship events under the "Amex Loves You" moniker. On one campus we might help fund a Pretenders and Bob Segar double headliner concert; on another, we might support an Amex Loves You film series or a comedy fest featuring a known headliner such as Steve Martin, Eddie Murphy, Richard Pryor, or Robin Williams. Because students were so open and responsive, the student card marketing program was fun to manage.

After a few years at American Express, inbound headhunter calls picked up in frequency and in possible fit. I generally eschewed these and explained that I was very happy at Amex for the time being. However, given my interest in the next new thing, one opportunity piqued my interest. This was with a Cambridge, Massachusetts-based startup called Softbridge Microsystems, Inc. The company was well financed, with two major VCs prominently represented on the capitalization table. Softbridge had several computer science wizards on the senior management team, all from nearby MIT.

The company planned to utilize its advanced "knowledge-based" algorithms to enable its users to generate valuable, mission-critical, bespoke reports. Over time, as the Softbridge system "learned" the practitioner's preferences and biases, it would overlay their unique approaches to create practice management deliverables. Softbridge's knowledge-based technology was an early, crude forerunner to artificial intelligence. Initially, the company planned to market its capabilities to financial planners. Once it dominated the financial planning market, Softbridge hoped to extend its reach—one vertical market at a time. The visual I had was of falling dominoes.

I was invited by David Adler, Softbridge's New York-based headhunter, to interview for the senior position of VP, Head of Marketing. I was to meet Russ Werner, the company's hard-charging COO, who would be in New York the following Tuesday. Russ had a goldfish look, pouty lips, and droopy eyes. He had traveled down from Cambridge that morning and had already met with four candidates to fill the final open position on the Softbridge senior management team.

Our conversation was a two-way dialogue; Russ spent as much time questioning me as he did selling me on the prospects for Softbridge. After about an hour, Russ began to discuss the general compensation package parameters, with particular emphasis on the potential value of the equity that would be made available to the successful candidate for the top marketing job. The hour flew by, and as we got up to leave, he let me know that he was keenly interested and that he would be in touch within the week.

That night I excitedly told Amy about the interview. Her reaction was positive, but a bit wary. She was reserving her full reaction for now since the odds of my getting the job were still low.

Two days later, I heard from David Adler, who had received a call from Russ Werner. Russ let David know that he was keen on me and wanted to arrange for me to meet key members of the team in Cambridge. This was very good news. Russ's compelling business vision had contributed to my growing desire to be selected for the position. There were a few questions that remained for me. Would Amy be willing to be uprooted? Would I find the compensation package sufficiently remunerative? Could I understand the company's culture and determine whether I would be a good fit? And, oh yes—would I actually receive a bona fide offer? I was getting way ahead of myself.

The following Wednesday, I took the shuttle from LaGuardia to Logan Airport and a cab toward Alewife off Route 2. The company was located on the second floor of a nondescript strip mall above a Josey's nail salon. It was a far cry from the American Express corporate headquarters, with its soaring granite and massive artwork too angular to soften the visitor's inescapable impression they had entered a cold, corporate den of power. If anything, Softbridge's quarters signaled struggle. Even the signage was in Magic Marker rather than etched in bronze.

Inside, I was struck by the mess: computers and computer parts on long fold-out tables, large boxes strewn throughout the open areas and in nearly every office, and multiple whiteboards with cryptic bullet points handwritten in varying colors. I also noted the high level of mobility of the managers and associates, freely walking to and from each other. This hive of activity indicated a culture attuned to teamwork and shared mission.

After spending time with the key staff members as well as with Mark Eisner, the company's enigmatic CEO, founder, and chief technology officer, Russ let me know that he thought it had been a very productive and full afternoon and that I would be hearing from him soon. In fact, he reached out the next day and offered me the position. We hashed out a generous compensation package that needed to be approved by Mark Eisner. Russ assured me that Mark's review would be perfunctory and that we should consider the package fully baked. He asked me to pay him another visit in Cambridge. I had already taken days off from Amex and was fearful that my colleagues would begin to put two and two together. Russ said he understood, and as it happened, he was hoping that I would be available to join him and a few Softbridge associates for dinner that Friday evening at 8 p.m. and to stay overnight, thereby not interfering with my current job.

This time, Amy was invited to join me and meet a few of my colleagues-to-be. Softbridge put us up at the Cambridge Hyatt Regency, and we dined in Harvard Square at Rialto, Jody Adams and Michaela Larsen's recently opened regional Italian smash hit, already recognized as a "best of" culinary award winner. Then on Saturday morning, Amy and I were given a tour of the Boston-Cambridge area so we could start to consider where we might look to move. Before our flight to Logan on Friday afternoon, Amy and I had spoken openly about the impending move. Much to my surprise, Amy was just as excited as I was. She understood that we would miss the proximity to family and friends, but she was also taken with the idea of striking out on our own. And, besides, Boston was near enough that we could drive to Westchester in roughly three hours.

Russ invited Jon Blum, Steve Sayres, and Judy Solerno to our Friday dinner. These three ran strategy, sales, and client services, respectively. Jon, an ex-Bain consultant, spent lunch working out at Gold's Gym, a short drive from our office. His outsized musculature distorted the proportions of his head and torso, such that his head appeared tiny and placed on the wrong body. He and his wife were friendly with the actress Geena Davis, who had recently made a little splash in *Tootsie*, her first movie role. Steve was affable, open, and genuine. He easily generated trust—the key element for any sales professional. Originally from South Boston, Judy was the salt of the earth. She could be tough on her client service reps but only when warranted. Judy was old-fashioned, thoughtful, and frequently brought in homemade cookies and brownies.

During dinner, I asked the group to give me a general picture of the prospective Softbridge client. Steve said I should see for myself and invited me to join him and several others in Chicago for the annual conference of the National Association of Personal Financial Advisors. Softbridge had taken an exhibit booth, where it provided materials and live examples of the system's capabilities. Further, as part of its sponsorship package, Softbridge EVP Jon Tepper was invited to present during one of the sessions, titled "The Business of Practice Management."

I decided not to make the trip in deference to my colleagues at Amex and all the things I needed to do in preparation for our move to Boston.

Chapter 9

Dirty Water

Russ urged me to find a suitable apartment as soon as possible. He was quite concerned that without me and my marketing toolkit in place, the momentum of new business opportunities might wither on the vine. And that momentum was very real. The National Association of Personal Financial Advisors, or NAPFA, conference was on its last day, and reports from our team manning the Softbridge booth indicated that the conference attendees were agog over the Softbridge system. We had built some interest prior to NAPFA, but the post-beta test version was unveiled at this conference. My colleagues had expected to sell ten systems and identify twenty highly interested prospective buyers at the conference. The actual sales were more than double these projections and represented the first revenues generated by the company. Happy days were here, and I was thankful to be an equity owner and senior manager at such an early stage, but there was much work to be done.

 I had given my notice to American Express, and after the

requisite two weeks, Amy and I spent a weekend in Boston looking at apartments. We narrowed our search to historic Beacon Hill and charming Back Bay, our preferred sections of the city. We found a snug, bowed apartment on Back Bay's St. Germain Street. This section of the Back Bay is part of a five-block no man's land across from the South Boston line. Each of the five streets is idyllically residential, but the small neighborhood was delineated by several large and ungracious buildings, including the hulking Church of Christian Science and the Back Bay Hilton, which was perpetually obscured by scaffolding and drop cloths. Softbridge put me up in a furnished corporate apartment on Beacon Street for the two weeks until the end of the month and the start of our new lease on the St. Germain apartment. Over the fortnight, Amy was busy in New York packing us up and arranging for the movers.

Those first few months in Boston were difficult. On the first day of our move, midway through unpacking, Amy and I decided to go out for a quick bite of dinner on Boylston Street. When we returned, we were met with the aftermath of a burglary. The perpetrators must have seen our movers complete their unloading and waited until we left our new apartment. Amy's clothes had been rifled through, and the burglars found her secret place for keeping excess cash and jewelry, including sentimental pieces from Amy's family. They got off with cash and thousands of dollars in jewelry, plus my high-performance Boston Acoustics speakers. It could have been much worse, but the feeling of being violated on our first night in our new home was not an auspicious start to our lives in Beantown.

Even more troubling was the sudden change in outlook for Softbridge. The product was now selling well, but the more systems we sold, the more we needed to visit our clients—many of whom were having problems with their new "mission-critical" system. We were the first approved reseller of the IBM PC, which enabled us to control the software configuration prior to shipping. The base PC in 1984 cost $6,000, about $20,000 in 2025 dollars. Considering its very limited power and storage capability, at least by today's standards, this was a significant investment for a one-to-five-person planning firm. Still, the PC was the only affordable choice for those planners who needed some form of automation to leverage their business. Our arrangement with IBM was that Softbridge's take on each IBM PC sold as part of a bundled package was 25% of the computer's retail price. This extra $1,500 revenue gave us some pricing flexibility. The 1984 fully bundled Softbridge system with the PC was priced at approximately $55,000. The problems should have been expected.

Conceptually, what our programming engineers had accomplished was remarkable. By entering relevant client data as well as answers to 87 questions posed to the planner, the computer could complete an entire, fully integrated financial plan reflecting the planner's key practice beliefs. The planner could also dial up or down the level of detail to include in the report, and correspondingly, the length of the plan. The guts of the plan relied on many thousands of calculations, which taxed—but at least on our in-house PCs didn't break—the system. Given the complexity of what was being accomplished, it's no wonder there were breakdowns in the hands of our clients, who were computer novices. The system might get 99.9 percent of the calculations right, but the final 0.1% might have a bug which resulted in the wrong bottom-line number.

It was all hands on deck, and I, too, was drafted into the service team. In the field, I was struck by the faith our clients had in me. They assumed I was a software engineer based on the little jargon I strategically used. I had been prepped by the real engineers and the content specialists whose domain expertise were input into the major sections of the output, including investments, tax, insurance, and trust & estates. Maintaining the excitement we had built in light of the disappointing early user experience was a significant challenge.

Amy and I had a number of visitors to our St. Germain apartment during the year we were there. My old Trinity and New York City roommate, Tim Ghriskey, stayed with us on the eve of his interview with Loomis Sayles, an old-line institutional money management firm headquartered in Boston with offices in ten different cities, including New York. Tim was hoping to get a job in the firm's equity research group. A month after his interview he was offered the position, which meant that Tim and his wife, Lisa, were en route northward. Our Boston circle was expanding.

Under horrific circumstances, Linda and Rob Moser—my sister and brother-in-law—stayed at our St. Germain apartment over a series of non-scheduled visits. Their third child, Susan, was born with a very large tumor on her sphincter muscles which protruded outward. None of this had been spotted on prenatal ultrasounds so it was a total shock. Robby, who was present during the delivery, fainted upon seeing the terrible growth. In the days following her delivery, Linda and Robby tried negotiating the complex and competitive world of New York City pediatric surgical specialists. Susan's case quickly became a must-have for these ambitious surgeons.

In that first week, my sister changed. Linda became a fierce, aggressive defender of her family and no longer acquiesced to points of view that didn't comport with what she believed was best for Susan. Convinced that the New York hospitals were more interested in burnishing their own reputations and managing their institutional risk, rather than Susan's survival, Linda and Rob opted to place her in the care of Dr. Hardy Hendren, who was affiliated with Boston Children's Hospital. Hendren was contacted by Linda and Robby's very good friends, Jimmy and Merrill Tisch, who were patrons of the hospital. Hardy Hendren was known as "Hardly Human" to the families and colleagues who saw him in action. In Susan's case, he literally created missing organs from Susan's other organs. We were not expecting a good outcome, and so these visits to Boston were generally suffused with a somber tone. But over a period of a few months, it became clear that Susan would make it. And that she has done. Some 40 years later, Susan continues to suffer bouts of severe stomach pain and has other complications that flare up from time to time, but she has made the most of her second chance at life. A graduate of Cornell and NYU Law School, her career has been impressive. Following her tenure as an associate at Proskauer, she is currently in line to become General Counsel of a large insurance company based in southern Connecticut. She is married, and although her condition prevented her from becoming pregnant, she and her husband, John, retained a gestational surrogate who successfully carried their adorable son, Wesley, to term.

Our Boston social life was taking shape. John Battle, my good friend from Trinity and St. A's, lived in Boston, where he worked as an architect. Through John, we met George Cole and his wife, Barbara. George was a graduate of Wesleyan and a classmate of John's at Harvard's architecture master's program. He was working for a real estate development firm when we first met. I became very close to these two wonderful friends. They were serious people who enjoyed meeting over a beer and discussing the state of politics, business news, the arts, and—in George's case—whatever gossip he had uncovered along the way. Both George and John were optimistic in their worldview and their demeanor. They embraced my offbeat sense of humor, and I could be totally myself with them. George and John became my trusted confidants over the course of my Boston period.

Our lease on the St. Germain Street apartment was approaching renewal. Instead of re-upping, Amy and I opted to move to a larger and better-located apartment on Dartmouth Street just off Beacon Street in the heart of Back Bay. Has it already been a full year since we first moved to Boston? Much had happened, most of which was good, some of which was not. Amy and I decided we should start a proper family—one that included children. Sadly, Amy miscarried twice, the second time on the eve of our departure for Westchester. The third time, however, was the charm, and on November 10, 1986, Max was born. He was named for Mighty Max Weinberg, the exacting drummer of Bruce Springsteen's E Street Band. After the delivery, I drove home to shower and change. Before returning to the hospital, I stopped at Tower Records to purchase Springsteen's just-released triple live album. When I got to the hospital, I learned that Amy had been dangerously bleeding out. Toni Walzer, her doctor, was livid that she hadn't been called in sooner by the nurses. Once Amy was stabilized and she was in the clear, I was thrilled to be a dad. I felt the weight of the moment. Just as a wedding elevates a loving relationship, the birth of a newborn—and particularly a first born—makes for a family. Max was followed by Ted in April of 1988 and then Molly in 1992.

The job with Softbridge had become a grind, especially given the likelihood that the company would need more time and dilutive financing to reach its two milestones: becoming cash flow positive and securing the top share of the market. So, when I received a call from a headhunter named Donald Samuels, I was open to discussing his client's opportunity. Don told me he was conducting a highly confidential search on behalf of his retainer client, a large private money management firm that had ten or eleven offices and was headquartered in Boston. "Oh, you must be working with Loomis Sayles," I said. He gasped. "How did you know?" I explained that Tim Ghriskey had stayed with me and my wife while he was in Boston to interview at Loomis. "Good karma," Don responded. "Let's get you in there as soon as possible." "Yes, let's," I agreed.

In short order I interviewed with Dugal Thomas, then Bob Kemp, President and CEO, and was soon on board. What a difference in job content and atmosphere from my strip mall experience at the struggling Softbridge. Loomis Sayles was located on two high floors in the gleaming One Financial Center building, which towered over South Station in the downtown business district. On my first day, I heard a knock on my office door. It was the shoeshine man that came around twice a week. Then, 10 minutes before 5 p.m., Dugal stopped by and let me know that he hoped I had a good first day and that he was leaving for the day. I went to the men's room, and when I returned to my office, I noticed that the entire place was dark. Fortunately, I had been given a key that afternoon or I would have been locked in until the cleaning crew arrived. Working for Loomis was not the worst thing I ever did.

The firm was a bastion of Protestant and Episcopalian sensibilities, and although I was one of only two Jews at the firm, I felt at home—just as I had in my waspy Trinity fraternity. The office was tastefully furnished, although not to my more contemporary taste. Its royal blue and brown tones emphasized the firm's long history, as did the choice of mahogany Chippendale furniture throughout the spacious entrance area and its adjacent meeting rooms. The walls were filled with large, wooden-framed maps, both nautical and Boston area-focused, as well as sepia-toned photos of former CEOs dating back to the 1920s, when Loomis Sayles was founded.

At 53, Dugal Thomas, my new boss, was 22 years my senior. I assumed he drank too much, given the combination of his essential tremor and facial rosacea. From the start he let me know that I was running the show as Director of Marketing. He had been given that title by Bob Kemp, who was the head of the firm. Dugal candidly explained that he was not interested in doing anything that kept him from his highly incentivized position selling and servicing Ken Heebner's clients and prospective clients. In the mid- and late eighties, Ken, via his CGM Fund, was recognized as either the number one or number two equity portfolio manager in the country. Fidelity's Peter Lynch was the other, more recognized growth stock manager. His fame was boosted by the Fidelity marketing machine that was focused on advancing Peter's Magellan Fund. Ken had a touch of paranoia about him and believed that in mid-December, as the sweepstakes for best full-year fund performance drew closer, Fidelity had someone rummage through his garbage to ascertain his current portfolio holdings. With that knowledge, they would be able to instruct the managers of other, less visible Fidelity mutual funds that were not managed by Lynch to sell off the names that overlapped with the CGM fund holdings and punish the share price of these securities. Of course, market manipulation is illegal, and Fidelity would not have risked its terrific reputation by engaging in such activity.

Dugal had the patience and offbeat smarts to thrive in Ken's orbit. He was fascinated with language and creative ways to exhibit the firm's intellectual property. On behalf of Dan Fuss, our other star portfolio manager who ran the fixed income side of the business, Dugal created a very different "pitch book." This was nothing more than a single piece of paper. On it were several hand-drawn horizontal lines with a few bubbles drawn in between the lines. At meetings with prospective clients, he would explain that the lines represented credit ratings, from the highest-quality bonds, rated AAA at the top of the page, to incrementally lower-quality bonds below that. The bubbles were individual bonds. He would point to the bottom bubbles and explain that they represented high-yielding securities, and, like lungfish, Dan's group thrived in deeper waters. These securities had the advantage of paying out at a higher yield while offering the potential for capital appreciation if and when the quality ratings improved and were upgraded. For many, this explanation demystified and clarified our approach to fixed income management.

Working with Ken Heebner was like working with a manic-depressive. He needed enemies from both within and without Loomis. His trusted team was limited to just a few people, including Dugal, Bob Kemp, Leslie Lake (his administrative assistant), and, to a far lesser extent, me. Paul Reeder, considered to be the most talented equity analyst in the firm, couldn't understand why he was on the outs with Heebner. It was simple: Ken Heebner strongly believed that analysts should analyze the companies they covered, which meant that they should research and provide information. It did not mean they should provide stock recommendations, and when they did, they were trespassing on the portfolio manager's hallowed ground. Paul would leave the firm and start his hedge fund, PAR, and do exceedingly well.

Another of Ken's demons was Ralph Verni, the head of The New England, a mutual life insurance company that owned a majority stake in Loomis. Ken and Bob gave me the thankless task of being the firm's go-between with the parent company. What that really meant was that I needed to stall, obscure, and obfuscate in as many creative ways as I could dream up. Even I began to enjoy stiff-arming Verni and his associates.

With a few years under my belt, Ken and I traveled to New York to meet with Frank Borelli the temperamental CFO of our client Marsh McLennan (aka, Marsh Mac). On the shuttle down, I noticed our meeting book included Marsh Mac as a sample holding. I wanted to make sure Ken was ready to discuss his rationale for owning the stock with the company's insiders. Ken said the bigger issue was that he had sold out of his position just a few days earlier and the stock had suffered accordingly. He said he wanted to "do a Watergate," and he started to rip out the offending page from our meeting book. I told him that was not the solution because we had already fedexed the presentation materials two days ahead of our meeting.

We were early and waited outside the board room. Frank

Borelli began to yell at the top of his lungs and although the walls were thick, we could clearly hear his ranting. Somebody was getting chewed out in a big way. When the door opened, I recognized Clive O'Connor, and judging from his ashen mien, he and his four colleagues had been victims of Borelli's venom. They were from Putnam, which at the time was owned by Marsh Mac. If that's how he treated colleagues, how would he deal with us?

Ken leaned over to me and told me "don't worry. Borelli won't know about our Marsh Mac stock sales. We're fine."

We were invited into the boardroom, and before we had taken our seats, a hostile Borelli asked in a booming, on-edge voice, "So, tell me, Ken, why you dumped our stock." Ken took a deep breath and, for the next hour, gave Borelli and a retinue of his acolytes a lesson on their own business. He identified and addressed their weaknesses. At first, I was concerned about Ken's temerity in challenging Borelli, but every issue raised by Ken was spot on.

After the first fifteen minutes, Borelli sent for his boss, the president of the company. Frank's subordinates by now knew to take detailed notes. After that performance, I realized we would never lose the Marsh Mac account for fear of losing Ken's business insights. Afterwards, I queried Ken on how he was able to wow everyone in the room. He confessed that, once he realized that Borelli and his team would likely be aware of his sale of Marsh Mac stock, he made it a point to have dinner the previous night with the number one-rated insurance analyst on Wall Street.

Ken and I were due to present in a finals competition hosted by NEPC, a major institutional consulting firm. The prospective client was Stop & Shop, the large northeastern grocery chain. At the last moment, Ken pulled out due to an issue with one of his holdings. That left me alone to face the eight men from Stop & Shop and Dick Charlton, the founder and CEO of NEPC. I went through our presentation and invited the group to feel free to stop me with any questions.

I was asked about Ken's investment in Texas Air. I explained Ken's thesis: that Frank Lorenzo, the airline's CEO, was a tough guy who would break the union's back, enabling the airline to become a formidable low-cost operator. I waited a beat and couldn't help but notice an atmospheric shift—a palpable heaviness in the air. It took me far too long to realize that this was a Taft-Hartley union pool of assets and that Dick and I were the only people in the room who were not union members. How could I be so stupid?

We didn't win the bake-off, and I was mighty embarrassed, but I never forgot the lesson: always know who you are speaking to. Ken loved the story and said he wished he had been a fly on the wall. Years later, when I was a client of NEPC in my dual role as head of the investment committee for the Union for Reform Judaism and investment committee member of the Reform Pension Board, Dick Charlton told me he never forgot my gaffe and that he and he and his colleagues still get a laugh out of the story.

Some time later, I received a call from IBM's Controller, Larry Zimmerman, who informed me that Big Blue planned to allocate $75 million to Ken. In the late eighties and early nineties, this was a very large allocation, and I told Larry that I was delighted to hear this news. They had only one request: would I ask Ken to reduce his already concentrated portfolio to just ten stocks?

I went to Ken's office to give him the good news. When I got to the part about reducing the number of holdings from his normal twenty to twenty-five names down to ten, he began to turn watermelon red. He was trying, and failing, to keep his cool. With clenched teeth he spat out "you tell those IBM fuckers I don't want their money. No one tells me how to manage a portfolio, no one!" So I called Larry and let him know that Ken would not deviate from his portfolio and that he treated all client portfolios in a similar manner. Zimmerman was disappointed, but later that week he reached out to me again. He told me he respected Ken's position and therefore the blue-chip company was shelving the provision regarding the concentrated ten-stock portfolio.

I went straight to Ken and enthused, "Good news! IBM's $75 million is a go and there are no longer any strings attached." Ken's reaction was vintage Heebner. He said "You failed me, Ralph. Did I not tell you to convey to them to go fuck themselves? That we don't want their filthy money? Call them back and use the following words exactly: 'Go fuck yourself.'"

Chapter 10

Looking Out the Window

It had been some years since the start of my employment with Loomis Sayles, and I was able to perform my job at a reasonably high level without breaking a sweat. Notwithstanding my work travel schedule, which took me out of Boston one to three days a week, this gave me the freedom to spend more time with Amy and the kids. Once Max's baby brother, Teddy, arrived, we made room for him in the larger apartment we had just moved into.

The apartment, situated on Marlborough Street off Exeter—near our former apartment on Dartmouth Street—had a grand, high-ceilinged parlor room that must have seen a few dances in its storied past. Its wainscoting was a rich, dark brown. Amy and I imagined that the house was once the home of one of the city's power-couple socialites. And while we didn't require dinner jackets and gowns, we did throw a few raucous parties there. Sadly, we never had the nerve to invite our next-door neighbors, The Cars frontman Ric Ocasek and his model wife, Paulina Porizcova, who took a liking to Max and Ted.

An added benefit to this move was that when my brother Michael and his wife, Anne moved to Boston for Mike's new job, they found an apartment only one block from us. This gave Max and Ted the chance to be with their cousins, Jake and Lucy. Likewise, it gave Amy and me the chance to be with Anne and Mike. More than a few people commented on the similarities between the oldest and youngest Sinsheimer brothers. Michael followed me to Camp Takajo, Trinity College, NYU Stern, and now Boston. Additionally, Anne and Amy had similar physical features. Both were fit, dark-haired, and brown-eyed. I always liked the idea that whatever I screwed up, Mike would be able to get a redo on my behalf.

Even before he was one year old, Max began to attend the "happy" place called Room for Children on Newbury Street. The owner, Cameron, was very sweet and attracted several college counselors to provide a loving and safe space—and an introduction to toddler socialization—for the very young kids in her care. It was there that Amy and I were befriended by Lois and Alan Green, whose sons, Nick and Ben, lined up with Max and Teddy age-wise. Max and Nick were very close, and we enjoyed Lois and Alan. Sometimes, in an amusing way, Alan would act as a caricature of himself. His expertise was in organizational behavior, and he spoke in corporate jargon. Often he would remind us that he was his own man, a sole practitioner, and he could "turn the key in the condo" and go sailing at any time. The man could drink his scotch, and we had many great evenings together.

When Loomis Sayles needed to replace its longtime CEO, it retained Heidrick & Struggles to identify candidates and oversee the search process. The successful candidate was Robert Murphy, the former CEO of insurance and investment giant Prudential. From day one, I sensed this would be a case of oil and water. As his first move, Murphy hired two executive assistants, whereas Bob Kemp, his predecessor, had never needed to inflate his importance by surrounding himself with the trappings of an exalted executive.

There was a subtle but important difference between the goals of becoming a small large company, and a large small company. Loomis had always looked askance at the former since it implied a hierarchical organization. No, Loomis was a flat, efficient, and profitable firm that hired people who would make an impact from day one. I had already started to refer to Murphy as the "summer intern" when he was terminated eight weeks into his tenure. The firm looked inside and named Don Shepherd, the very popular head of our successful Pasadena office and a man with no ego issues.

Don agreed to take the CEO position but didn't want to move east to Boston. Instead, he asked me if I wanted the CEO's office. I replied, "Of course not. It's your office regardless of the frequency of your visits to Boston. When I become CEO, I'll take it," I quipped. Don said he was a pragmatist, and if I could deal with the occasional disruption of having to find a swing office during his quarterly visits, the CEO's office was all mine.

The office was huge and beautifully decorated. The best feature was the 270-degree, uninterrupted views out of the contiguous giant windows that wrapped around most of the office. The spectacular panorama included a full sweep of Boston

Harbor and, further out on the horizon, the airplane takeoffs and landings at Logan. Max's teacher relayed a story to me: each student was asked to tell the class what their parents did for a living. The answers included doctors, teachers, bankers, and so on. Apparently, Max was a little hesitant but finally and firmly said, "My dad looks out the window." Not a bad answer for my daydreaming days, which included new entrepreneurial urges.

These urges were honed during my visits and phone calls with my friend Ken Rothstein, as well as lunches with my former roommate and current Loomis Sayles colleague, Tim Ghriskey. Tim and I spent many of our weekly lunches considering a future in which we ran our own investment firm. However, once Tim was transferred to the Loomis Sayles New York City office, those discussions were back-burnered. Ken Rothstein stepped into the void, and then some.

Ken had noted a nascent trend at select restaurants—chiefly in New York, Los Angeles, and Chicago—that were serving gourmet pizzas with high-quality and sometimes unusual toppings. What was not available was a gourmet-quality frozen pizza. Ken believed he had an uncanny ability to spot the next big consumer "thing," but he had neither the experience nor the aptitude to create and execute a business plan. Given the very large total addressable market for frozen pizza and the undeniable growing trend of restaurant gourmet pizza, I thought it was a very good idea—but that Ken was not equipped to pull it off. To his credit, he recognized this and asked me to help him create a business plan that might be an effective tool for raising the money necessary to move forward. I told him I would try to do so, but that I wouldn't be sucked into the project.

After completing my research on the frozen pizza market

and the challenges and opportunities a new entrant might face, I informed Ken that he would need to first create and test the product, find a co-packer to potentially make the product in large batches, secure funding for the first phase of the company's life, identify a CEO with deep experience in the food business, and, lastly, sell in meaningful quantities to at least one important, recognizable customer. Ken knew that each of these milestones was necessary, yet very difficult to achieve. He then asked me to continue helping him, but as an equal partner. My fear was that this would prove to be too big a distraction and might compromise my day job with Loomis. I told Ken that against my better judgment I would continue working with him, but only for six months.

Over that period, we were able to attain all the objectives I had laid out. We each put $40K into the company coffers and hired two different food technologists—one for the toppings and the other for the crust. Moisture migration had long been the bane of frozen pizza consumers; it severely compromised the texture and flavor of the pie. We engaged a group from the American Institute of Baking in Kansas to create a crust that would be far less susceptible to the moisture problem. Closer to home, Ken had selected food scientist Guy Livingston of Dobbs Ferry to create an initial set of four toppings.

We made a sample run of one hundred pizzas and froze them. We also bought a large toaster oven with which we served samples to people who could help us reach our milestones. This included frozen food buyers at large supermarkets, venture capitalists, co-packers, and food industry executives. The product was universally praised, and we were given more encouragement than we needed. To further refine and telegraph the product's positioning, we trademarked the name Upper Crust, which was owned by our company, Quintessence, Inc. We created artwork for the pizza's packaging and configured six boxes to show during our various meetings.

Having a reliable co-packer nailed down—with guarantees regarding its ability to maintain quality and throughput at high volume levels and within pre-specified unit costs—was vitally important. We visited scores of bakery operations and food co-packers before deciding to tap Ariston, whose main operations were near Fort Dix in New Jersey. In our search for our anchor customer, we visited several supermarket chains and a few large single-store operations, as well as some high-profile people who might give us valuable advice about selling to the chains. These ranged from the Balducci family in Greenwich Village to Murray Lender, the frozen bagel maven, in Connecticut.

We met with Joe Disco, the frozen food buyer for A&P, at the time a major U.S. supermarket chain that was owned by Germans and run by Brits. Unbeknownst to Ken and me, the company—which included the A&P, Food Emporium, Pathmark, Waldbaum's, and Super Fresh store lines—had recently decided to emphasize its private label brand, in keeping with the British view that store brands were generally higher in quality than those of independent, packaged food companies. The chain's Master Choice products would be given more visibility and shelf space.

Disco took two bites of his heated Upper Crust slice and picked up the phone. He was speaking with his boss, Peter Gorman, Senior Executive Vice President, and telling him he should come to his office as soon as possible. Gorman soon entered. There was a smug swagger to him. He wore a fedora and a blue suit with almost garish bold stripes. His shoes were from John Lobb. At Joe's urging, he sampled our pizza. Gorman indicated his total satisfaction with the product but had no interest in seeing our plans or the artwork we had commissioned for Upper Crust. No, Peter's interest was strictly in Master Choice, the private label business for which he was responsible. He gave us the background about the line and the chain's strategic imperative to differentiate itself via its value and quality. Peter then said they were looking for the second of two "hero products" to prove their claim that the Master Choice store-owned brands offered better quality at fairer prices. The idea that the only gourmet frozen pizza in the U.S. would be under the Master Choice line was tantalizing to him and Disco. We agreed to provide the product at a specified price if certain volume requirements were met. Further, we were open to a three- or six-month exclusive if A&P would increase our pricing.

Although there were still some details to be completed, Gorman asked us to take the sample product to London, where the preferred Master Choice food stylist-photographer was located. Ken convinced him that the product had to be handled with kid gloves and might not fare well over a long journey. Therefore, we (and our pizza stored with dry ice) should take the Concorde. Incredibly Ken's suggestion was approved.

Then, upon our return, Gorman asked us to travel to Chicago for the annual food show at McCormick Place. There, we were interviewed by several industry magazines. I was torn between being thrilled and worrying that things were getting beyond our control. We hadn't actually confirmed with our targeted CEO, and we would need a lot of money—several million dollars—to be assured of fulfilling the large numbers we expected from A&P.

Ken's value to Quintessence was his initial insight into the opportunity, his tireless efforts to secure initial meetings, and his role as baker and server of the Upper Crust pizzas during our meetings. He knew what he didn't know and ceded everything else to me, particularly if it required an intimate understanding of our business plan. One of the recurring challenges we had was that Ken's superpower—his chutzpah, which enabled us to get into any door no matter how firmly it was shut—could be offset by his quirky behavior. This often manifested in his unnerving habit of being late to meetings and checking repeatedly for things he might have left behind, which fed into his tardiness.

A difficulty we faced was the chicken-or-egg nature of our goals. A VC would need to know who was going to run the company, and conversely, a food executive would only sign up if there was enough capital already invested in the start-up. We offered Bill Dordelman the CEO position. Bill had previously run the frozen Bird's Eye food division of General Foods, and his résumé was perfect for what we intended. At the same time, we began a dialogue with the venture capital arm of First Boston, with whom we circled three million dollars. Incredibly, we hadn't yet dropped any of the balls we were juggling.

With the letter of intent from A&P in hand, Dave Billings from First Boston and Bill Dordelman only needed to meet with the co-packer, Ariston in southern New Jersey near Fort Dix. Ken drove the four of us to Wrightstown and parked in the visitors' lot. We all got out of the car and shut the doors. Kenny walked around the car twice, checking and rechecking every door to make sure they were locked. At that moment, I wondered if he would make a third round. It didn't matter—I had already seen the glance between Bill and Dave that told me that we were dead in the water. Sadly, Ken's condition had cost us the opportunity.

I spent the next several weeks dealing with the unwinding of our—or at least, my—activity, while Ken tried to breathe life into the project. It had been six months, and I needed to move on.

Chapter 11

Eureka! Get Yer Red Hot Beer Here

During this time, Amy and I moved to a house in the Brookline part of Chestnut Hill, very close to the Park School. Park was a private grade school that was one of the best day schools in the Boston area. I believe the application-to-acceptance ratio was no higher than 20%. It was a very exclusive group of families that were part of the Park community, and those who wanted in used a variety of strategies to boost their chances. Since we were never exposed to frantic competition around school admissions, we didn't have a strategy. Instead, five-year-old Max led the way.

On the morning of his interview Max had a terrible cold with a runny nose. Park indicated we should come in as planned, and so we did, with Max ever the trooper. He was his usual thoughtful, empathetic self as he interacted with the other tiny candidates, including a sweet little boy named Jay Manzi. While the kids played, we chatted with two of the admissions officers, discussing the school's philosophy and approach. We loved everything we saw and heard. Guileless Amy, instead of playing it cool, effused to the admissions staff and asked outright, "How can we get Max a place at Park?" Apparently, in our case, those were the magic words, and even before we had acquired the new Chestnut Hill house, Max was on his way to Park School, trailblazing for his brother Ted and new baby sister Molly, who would both be enrolled at Park once they reached the required age.

It was true that the Park School was a community. We made many satisfying and important friendships over the years as involved parents of Park students. These included Bill Hunter, an attorney, and Jill, his wacky and fun wife. Jill was very close to her mother and called her every night. When her mother died, Jill made sure to bury her with a phone in the coffin. Jill adored pink flamingos, and she had thirty-five neon pink, plastic, long-legged facsimiles "grazing" on her lawn. It was not easy to be a neighbor of the Hunters.

Another Park couple we spent time with was Donald Miller and his wife, Cricket Goldwyn. Donald was a very laid-back epidemiologist, and Cricket was part of Hollywood royalty as the "G" in MGM and the sister of actor/director Tony Goldwyn. Her first marriage to Gary Burton, the great Grammy Award-winning vibraphonist, resulted in divorce following Gary's announcement that he was homosexual. Amy and I were also quite friendly with Gary and Carol Moss. Gary was meticulous in his grooming and his dress, which normally featured an edgy, all-black outfit. He was from Chicago and one of the top executives at a national advertising agency.

Jim Manzi, a one-time classics scholar with a very sharp

and ironic sense of humor, was married to Glenda, but by the time we left the Boston area, their marriage was disintegrating. Jim was a former McKinsey consultant who became Chairman and CEO of spreadsheet software leader Lotus Development Corporation. When Lotus was sold to IBM for roughly $3.5 billion, Jim stayed on for a short time as was required of him. Newly enriched and not at all enamored of IBM Chairman Lou Gerstner, his new boss, he resigned from the company as soon as he was contractually allowed. He would become the non-executive Chairman of Thermo Fisher Scientific, a $250 billion market cap life science technology company.

On two occasions, Jim hosted me, Donald, and Bill for a "boys'" weekend at his homes in Cotuit and Vermont. The latter was a 12,000-plus-square-foot lodge that I thought of as his Xanadu. On a weekend at Jim's Cotuit house, we finished playing cards and still had a meaningful amount of drinking ahead of us. Donald had brought with him a six-pack of Crazy Ed Chilleen's Red Hot Chili Pepper beer. We all tried it and agreed it was the only beer we had ever tasted that left you thirstier than before you drank it.

We began a spirited discussion about the beer's merits and potential to extend the quirky brand name to other products. At about 2:30 on Sunday morning, when we were ready to call it a night, Jim turned to me and said, "If Crazy Ed Chilleen is willing to sell his small company, I will back the acquisition, and we can have some fun." Later that day, after we'd all gotten some sleep, Jim reiterated his comment. The beer was based in Carefree, Arizona, home to The Boulders, one of my favorite resorts. I offered to fly out to visit Chilleen later that week. Jim said, "Go for it," and so I did.

I vividly remember entering Crazy Ed's bar off a dusty road. To the left of the bar was a large room in which the brewing equipment and ingredients were housed. The place was quiet, with just one man sweeping up and a bartender drying beer glasses. The back screen doors were held open with heavy rocks. I asked for Ed and the bartender nodded toward the back. I stepped outside and there was Crazy Ed, sitting on a fold-out chair that had lost a few slats but looked stable enough. Ed was a short, gray-bearded man with a beer drinker's belly. Over his formidable gut, he wore a T-shirt bearing an image of a muscular animated chili pepper looking down menacingly at a cowering lime. The caption above the illustration read, "Limes are for wimps. Try Crazy Ed's chili beer."

Ed and I had talked in advance of my visit, so I had a better sense of his business and he understood the purpose of our meeting. The company only had revenues of $2 million. The beer was sold in 16 countries and 32 states. It didn't take a genius to recognize how easy it would be to improve the business by limiting distribution to just a few states while repositioning the brand.

Ed admitted that he could use an injection of cash and business advice and that he would be open to changes in the direction of the company. But he let me know, in his gruff barking way of speaking, that he would only sell up to 49% of the company. I reported back to Jim, Bill, and Donald, and we all agreed there was no way we would be beholden to Chilleen. With that decided, we all fessed up to the fact that just because it was unique didn't mean the beer wasn't terrible.

After ten years with Loomis Sayles, I was ready to move on. I was still happy at the firm, but my foray into gourmet frozen pizza—and my flirtation with purchasing chili beer—suggested I needed something new. I had been introduced to Andrew Mann by Cameron, the owner of Room for Children on Newbury Street. Cameron occasionally babysat our kids and was dating Andrew casually. Andrew leaned on me for advice as he and Mark Massey— two young, highly respected equity analysts— contemplated jumping from their jobs at mutual fund giant Fidelity. Once they established Eureka!, Mark and Andrew continued to seek me out for thoughts on management-related issues, especially on new business strategies. I was enjoying these conversations and over the course of a few months, I got to know both Mark and Andrew, and they, me. So, when the two of them invited me to become the third and equal general partner of the new firm, I accepted.

Andrew was from San Francisco and was aggressively sharp. Just before I came on board, he attended a semiconductor analyst conference where Andrew Grove of Intel was the keynote speaker. Andrew was able to sit next to Grove at lunch. As he often did, he peppered the CEO with a series of questions that demonstrated his command of the key leverage points and trouble spots Grove would need to attend to. By dessert, Grove asked Andrew to send him new account paperwork, and he became an investor in our fund.

Mark was from Richmond, Virginia, where his family was well known. The Massey family's foundation was the backbone of the city's charitable giving, and the Massey name is attached to many Richmond streets and buildings. Their significant wealth came from the family's energy business, particularly its coal holdings. A.T. Massey founded the company in 1920, first as a coal brokerage, and beginning in 1945, as an operator. Mining for coal is not for the faint of heart. It's dirty and dangerous. Over the years, the company faced an array of litigation, primarily related to its poor environmental and safety records. Mine explosions killed a number of Massey workers. The company was also the target of a United Mine Workers strike, which sought to redress the poor working conditions, stinting compensation, and unsafe environmental practices. Although never admitting to any charges, there seemed to be no doubt that Massey was chronically negligent. Cynics intimated that the large family foundation was funded to provide whitewash and the appearance of pure-hearted philanthropy. That was a strong possibility.

The Eureka! hedge fund generated terrific performance but very little in assets. Upon joining, my role was twofold: to screen for small companies with certain growth-oriented characteristics so that Mark and Andrew had a pool of potential new ideas to research more closely, and to formulate and execute on a plan to bring in new business. After my initial few months becoming intimately acquainted with my partners' investment approach, I created a brochure which likened Eureka! to a coatimundi—a racoon-like mammal known for foraging grubs obscured by brush, dirt, or leaves. The brochure elicited derisive laughter from one or two people, including my broker father-in-law, but I was unfazed and felt it was a very good investment for Eureka! It forced us to articulate what we did, how we did it, how we had performed, and why we believed Eureka!'s outperformance would continue.

When we met with Beth Delalla, the head of equity manager research at the prominent institutional consulting firm

RogersCasey, I noticed that she had our brochure open on her desk with key sentences underlined and handwritten notes scribbled in the margins. She told us that the brochure had caught her attention. She praised it for its clarity and forceful explanation and defense of our investment approach. She also liked the art and layout, as well as the creative use of metaphor in our writing, a bold tactic she had never seen in our conservative industry. After an hour of Q&A on Eureeka!'s capabilities and its risk management process, she told us she would be placing our fund on their approved list and that we should be prepared to present to several of the firm's large clients. Her one concern was that we might not be able to maintain our edge if we got too big. I said that we believed that at $1.5 billion we would need to consider soft-closing the fund. Beth asked if we would be willing to reserve some of our capacity for RogersCasey clients, in the $200–300 million range. I answered that we would consider doing so if and when the consultancy directed $50 million to our fund—and that the capacity we promised would only be available for a year. In any event, it looked like we were on the verge of breaking through and were ready to play in the big leagues.

On the heels of our RogersCasey visit, I secured a meeting with Rudy Javits, who worked in the investment office at Mount Holyoke College. Rudy invited me and my partners to his office. Apparently, the endowment staff had been following us via my quarterly letters for the past year, and they were intrigued.

The morning of our Mount Holyoke visit, the three of us met at our office before traveling to the college for our 3 p.m. meeting. Andrew was a bit late, which annoyed me because we needed the time to prepare. At 9 a.m., he walked in rolling a TV and VHS player. Mark and I looked at each other blankly.

Andy smiled, turned on the TV, and just before hitting "play," he said, "Gentleman, this is a red-letter day in the life of Eureka! Let us sally forth and conquer." And with that he cued up a scene from *Glengarry Glen Ross*.

On the screen, David Mamet's real estate salesmen were being verbally and cruelly abused by Howard, their boss, played masterfully by a scene-stealing Alec Baldwin. Baldwin's character Howard rips into Shelley "the Machine" Levene (Jack Lemmon) with an inhuman venom and forbids Shelley from drinking the firm's viscous, day-old cold coffee. "Coffee's for closers!" he repeatedly barks. "A.I.D.A.—Attention, Interest, Decision, Action. ABC—Always Be Closing!" If Andrew was looking to land a bolt of lightning, it was a good try. Better than a good try, it was the first time in the year since we opened for business that the three of us could envision an exciting and very profitable future for Eureka! and its general partners. I gently reminded Andrew that this was to be our first meeting with the endowment's manager research team, and the best we could hope for was an invitation back to meet with the college's CFO, Lou Morrell. As for my partner, Mark, he seemed more uncomfortable than upbeat at the exhortations of Alec Baldwin.

We were early to our Mount Holyoke meeting. Rudy was still in a conversation with one of his external investment managers but quietly tiptoed to the door and in a hushed voice apologized for keeping us waiting and told us that he looked forward to our discussion. Fifteen minutes later, we were called into the conference room. As we had done at RogersCasey, we reviewed our growth-oriented approach to investing in micro- and small-cap companies. The meeting was a success. Not only did we get an invitation to return in two weeks, Lou Morrell—the college's iconoclastic CFO—stopped in for ten minutes and indicated that he would be sure to attend our next meeting in a fortnight when we returned to South Hadley.

Once we were back in the car with the doors shut, and no one could overhear us, I whooped. I was in an extremely good mood. Everything was clicking into place. Andrew shared my optimism; he rated the presentation a nine-and-a-half out of ten. Of course, to earn a perfect ten, we would have had to close the Mount Holyoke endowment right then and there. Mark had been uncharacteristically quiet.

When I returned to the office the next morning, I picked up a voicemail message from Bill Davidson of Wilshire Associates, the behemoth Los Angeles-based investment consultancy. Bill alluded to his role running a groundbreaking new institutional product: emerging manager research and search. It was exactly the kind of opportunity Eureka! had been hoping for.

The next morning, Andrew and I both arrived at the office early with a renewed sense of purpose. When Mark arrived, he told us we needed to talk. He apologized several times, his eyes welling up, and then dropped the bombshell: "I can't do this. I need to take a different path." Mark announced that he was leaving the firm. He had been increasingly wary of investing on behalf of mid-to-large institutions. Oddly, it was our growing success that triggered this crisis of faith. Mark recognized that we were a few meetings away from establishing a more profitable and recognizable firm, but that is exactly what he now feared. He was no longer interested in being beholden to clients and their consultants. Rather, he wanted to invest his own money and to change the direction of his career to the nonprofit world. Mark planned to work for or create his own better version of

GuideStar, the de facto leader in the aggregation and dissemination of key financial data of 501(c)(3) accredited charitable organizations. He had ideas to enhance the service—none of which I gave a damn about.

I asked how long he had been thinking about this move? Did he know he was effectively pulling the plug on the firm? I told him that when I made the leap from Loomis Sayles to join Eureka!, the last risk I thought I would need to guard against was that one of my partners would become scared of *succeeding*. Andrew wanted to continue on, but I knew that it was too late. That view was confirmed for me when I spoke to several of our most promising leads.

My focus shifted to job hunting, and much to Amy's displeasure, the net I threw was wide enough to include New York City firms. We had built a lovely life in Boston, and I understood and shared Amy's trepidation at the thought of moving away.

Chapter 12

The Glickenhaus Bridge

Seth Glickenhaus was a legend in the money management business. In his mid-nineties, he carried on faithfully the precepts of Graham and Dodd's value approach to investing. Graham and Dodd had many devotees, including Warren Buffet and other notable investors. The pair made a compelling case for considering the current market valuation of a stock versus its intrinsic value. They provided a roadmap for determining intrinsic value and for assessing how current stock prices compared to historical norms. To reach these values, Graham and Dodd-style investors employed a wide array of formulas, weighted differently depending on the industry in question. For example, a real estate investment in the commercial or residential sectors might call for an understanding of the company's price-to-free-cash-flow multiple, since the business is centered on generating cash yield via rental payments. Other investments might require a focus on price-to-sales.

Value investing stands in direct contravention to growth

investing, the latter embraced by Ken Heebner, Peter Lynch, and many others. The growth investor looks to ferret out companies that appear overpriced by conventional metrics, but whose future earnings power is underappreciated or misunderstood. Often, growth investors identify catalysts they believe will provide a lift to the prospects of the company they are considering.

Growth investors far outperformed value investors during the nineties, a decade characterized by the rise of the internet and the personal computer. As it often does, the yawing differential in performance between these two approaches created a distortion that was addressed in stunning fashion by the dot-com bust. From the very early aughts until 2008, a reversion to the mean occurred and style leadership shifted from growth to value. Another cyclical comeuppance will reoccur now that growth has outperformed its value counterparts for over a decade, rewarding mega-cap technology companies handsomely in the process.

Seth hired me as an institutional marketer. I was to work alongside Don Deutch, who had been at Glickenhaus & Company for a little over three years. Don had beady, mistrusting eyes that appeared even shiftier when he squinted. He sported a perpetual five o'clock shadow and a chin that jutted out menacingly. He was the most vile, hateful, and evil man I have ever worked with. He cared not a whit about his colleagues—particularly me, whom he viewed as competition. A true psychopath, Don morphed into a treacly, fawning yes man around Seth. On those rare occasions when we were both in a prospective client meeting, he dominated the discussion and poured honey on the prospect in a totally transparent and nauseating attempt to gain favor. He was also secretive, and I often caught him at my desk, no doubt looking for any contact information that would allow him to steal my relationships.

The office was not conducive to private conversation, so I began lining up meetings with some of the large Bermuda-based reinsurance companies I had previously worked with. Reinsurers typically have very limited staff but very large pools of capital to allocate. My idea was to entice Seth to travel with me. He agreed to do that and did me one better. He brought with him his lovely wife Sara and told me I should take Amy.

Prior to our arrival on the island, I had several discussions with Ann-Marie Gagnon, the Chief Investment Officer of PartnerRe. She oversaw $6 billion in assets, all managed externally. Ann-Marie was an impressive woman and very likeable. A single parent, she was extremely dedicated to her work. On the eve of our departure, she let me know how much she looked forward to meeting Seth, whom she had heard so much about. She then disclosed that PartnerRe had just signed a letter of intent and would be acquiring another reinsurer which would give her another $5 billion to invest. She was signaling to me that a meaningful piece was on reserve for Seth, pending of course the outcome of our meeting.

The two couples—Seth and Sara and Amy and me—had a very pleasant dinner together in Hamilton. I could tell that Amy adored Sara, and she let me know how much she looked forward to touring around the island together with her while Seth and I had our meetings the next day. Before we parted for the night, I exhorted Seth to be on his best behavior at our meeting with Ann-Marie. "A large mandate is ours to lose," I told him. All you need to do is breathe and smile. Maybe discuss one of our holdings. That's it."

The next morning, following our meeting at Swiss Re, we walked the two blocks to PartnerRe. Ann-Marie greeted us warmly and sat us across from her desk. She complimented Seth on his stellar reputation and his superior investment performance record. The nonagenarian nodded to Ann-Marie, opened his mouth, and said, "You know, Miss Gagnon, I would like to hire more women in my firm, but they just get pregnant and leave." I waited two beats in the hope that Seth would amend his comment or indicate it was a poor attempt at humor and apologize. But this old timer spoke his mind. Ann-Marie was stunned and angry but didn't call Seth out. She simply said that this was an unusual statement given the advances that women have made in the workplace.

Between Seth's unenlightened response to Ann-Marie—which cost me a large prospect—and the antics of my bitter enemy Don "The Terrible" Deutsch, I was unhappy and needed to find a firm that better suited me. Exacerbating my anxiety around my troublesome job situation was Amy's intransigence about moving the family back to the New York area. I fully understood why she resisted uprooting Max, Ted, and Molly. We had made a nice life for ourselves. Lots of very close friends, near enough to Westchester and our families to travel down on any weekend and far enough away that we weren't overrun by anyone. However, the reality was that I had a much better chance of restarting my career in New York than I did in Boston. As it was, to work at Glickenhaus, I was commuting from Boston each week and staying with my parents in Scarsdale. This was neither acceptable nor tenable. I needed to have my wife and children with me and not erode the loving family unit that we were.

So, I acted boldly—some would say I did so at my peril—and bought a house without Amy's input. The house in Katonah was off a three-mile dirt road and had the feel of a rural retreat, particularly since the lawn backed into a large nature preserve that guaranteed our privacy. Yet it was commutable to New York and located in a family-oriented, close-knit neighborhood. Situated on over four sloping acres, the single-level 1960s ranch has a great room notable for its soaring ceiling and stone wall fireplace. In time, the house would prove to be a prescient choice.

Amy was shocked when I told her what I had done, but she said she finally understood that we were really going to move. I would miss friends and confidants, John Battle and George Cole and the other good friends we had made in the area, but I had deep conviction that we were taking the right next step. We stayed a few days in Bermuda and then flew home to Boston. It was April Fools' Day when we departed Bermuda. The previous day the temperature in Boston had reached the mid-60s, but a cold front arrived, bringing one of the biggest snowstorms in Boston's history, and the most snow to ever fall in April: roughly 26 inches, at times at a rate of 3 inches per hour.

Because of the storm, our flight was rerouted to LaGuardia Airport. It occurred to me that with Logan closed for the foreseeable future, I should take this opportunity to rent a car and show Amy our new house in Katonah. What I hadn't considered was that with the snow, our yard, patio, and the long dirt road—normally so idyllic—had lost their Edenic charm. The storm had also knocked out power, so there were no working lights in the house, and with the snow clinging to our oversized windows and skylights, the entire place was shrouded in darkness. I could tell Amy was not exactly buoyed by what she saw. Happily, she had other chances to fall in love with the house—and in very little time, she did.

While continuing to work for Seth Glickenhaus, I contacted Morris Offit to begin my nascent job search. Prior to starting his own firm, Morris had been part of the Salomon Brothers senior management team. He was from Baltimore, where he first learned how to read a room—who had the power and who had the money. If someone came up to him who wasn't of interest (read: no power, no money), Morris would expertly shake the interloper's hand while simultaneously leading them away by the elbow before either of them had uttered a word. He had an uncanny way of closing business without being at all promotional. Instead of asking for the business, he simply looked to be helpful. Morris was a salesman par excellence, and I learned a lot from him.

Morris invited me to have breakfast with him and Wallace Mathai-Davis at his office. Wallace, the Chief Operating Officer of OFFITBANK, was generally regarded as the dark side of the firm. Morris relied heavily on his counsel. Wallace was an intriguing character. There was something about him that raised my antenna. He was naturally conspiratorial, and he sometimes made it a practice to whisper in the ear of some temporarily favored soul who was in the middle of a conversation with another colleague. Wallace had impeccable credentials: he was an economic sociologist and had a Ph.D. and M.A. from Princeton University. He graduated summa cum laude with a B.A. in philosophy from Notre Dame, where he also held a national Defense Fellowship for Soviet Studies. He was married to Prema Mathai, who had studied in Delhi and earned a doctorate in education from Harvard. Her career focused on advancing women's and children's health, and she served as the executive director of the Young Women's Christian Association, the leading provider of contraception in the world. Neither Wallace nor Prema was lacking in intelligence.

By any measure the breakfast meeting at OFFITBANK was a home run. Morris's office was on the 29th floor of 520 Madison Avenue, a premier building off 52nd street. Walking into the office, it was clear that the interior design team knew what they were doing. I later discovered that the "look" was Wallace's—he oversaw the tradesmen who actualized his vision. The office environment was one of the firm's great assets and contributed to its culture. I was struck immediately by the exquisitely tasteful use of Hawaiian Koa for the wood paneling as well as for the large boardroom table. With its warm golden and burnt sienna tones, wavy grains, and ribbon-like streaks, the koa served a second purpose; to ingeniously camouflage the front closets and cabinets. For a first-time visitor, there was practically no way to know anything was behind the paneled walls. Special carpeting, pale tan and simply patterned with very small green squares, added to the sumptuous front of the house. This public area included the boardroom, with large windows affording a western view; a small sitting room with a settee and two wingback chairs, and between them a small oval mahogany table with periodicals neatly ordered; and Morris's office. Mary Walsh, Morris's longtime, ever-gracious receptionist, was also stationed in the front portion of the office.

As for the content of our discussion, Morris and Wallace spent most of the time querying me about the programs I had put in place at my previous firms and whether I thought any of them might be helpful to OFFITBANK. It began to dawn on me that Morris was considering hiring me, an exciting and welcome development. He called me the next morning to say he would like to do just that and to come up with a mutually satisfactory compensation package. It felt good to complete my job search before it had truly begun.

During the first few weeks of my employment, it became clear that my new colleagues had been given a picture of me that was more flattering than I deserved. I felt sure I would let them down. Mary Walsh had dubbed me "the young Morris," which didn't help ease the pressure. The firm was serious in its purpose and still managed to be quite convivial. I generally liked my new colleagues and got to know several of them very well.

Joe Giglia was a wild card and could be a lot of fun. He was the quintessential hot-blooded Italian American, prone to flashing his anger or raising his voice at inappropriate times. He lived near me in Waccabuc, and we spent time together playing golf and trading notes on the state of the market. More often than not, he had someone to complain about. I envied the way he could start his day with a clean desk, respond to some of our largest clients, handle projects for Wallace or Morris, and manage to leave the office at 5 o'clock sharp with a similarly uncluttered desk.

Although Steve Blitz had a bigger-than-warranted ego and gave some of us the sense that he believed he was smarter than his colleagues, he was a good guy. He had been tapped by Morris to act as our in-house economist, and he penned an above-average monthly outlook letter. He had a bulbous Carl Malden nose, kinky hair, and a New York City borough accent. I picture him sitting at his desk or in a bar shrugging his shoulders, raising his eyebrows, and saying "Whatevah, what difference does it make?"

Until he divorced and moved back to Manhattan, Steve lived in the Edgemont section of Scarsdale, near another colleague, Scott Einhorn. Scott was a sports loving, fabulous dad. He had clearly chosen to focus on his twin boys, with whom he was totally smitten. He coached their baseball team and was quite serious about keeping stats and being an overall booster.

My office neighbors included Steve Wells and Albert Bellas, both about ten years my senior. A polio survivor, Steve was an Andover and Princeton graduate and became a trust and estates lawyer at Cadwalader, the oldest law firm in the country, founded in 1792. Steve was one of the most verbal people I knew. He had a prodigious vocabulary and was in full command of it. This was a mixed blessing because, although his communication skills were an advantage on balance, some people were put off by the length of his oratory and his occasional use of "fancy" words. Steve combed his hair slicked back and wore investment banker-style suspenders. Sadly, he was the whipping boy for Wallace Mathai-Davis, who could cruelly chew him out at the slightest provocation.

Albert Bellas had a compelling CV and a winning personality. He earned degrees from Yale University and the University of Chicago Law School. He worked as an intern in the Kennedy White House. His family, who were of Greek descent, owned several lucrative beer and liquor distributorships in Ohio. Albert's identical twin brother, Michael, became one of the country's leading experts on the marketing of beverages, both alcoholic and non-alcoholic. Before joining OFFITBANK, Albert was an investment banker and rose through the ranks of several leading firms. At Shearson, Albert was a member of the Board of Directors and was also charged with investing partner capital. His disposition was as shiny as his bald head. This, along with his broad, toothsome smile, led to his popularity.

Albert was an aficionado of modern and classical dance, and he married Kaye Mazzo, one-time prima ballerina for George Balanchine and head of faculty at the School of American Ballet, where Albert served as Chairman. In the early months following Sandy Weil's takeover of Shearson, Albert was called to see Sandy in his office at the top of the Financial Trade Center. Sandy asked him to take a seat, then laid into him. "Albert, I know what you're doing, and I want you to stop it. This organization cannot, and will not, condone extramarital activities. You know I think the world of Kaye. For now, this is between us, but if I learn you haven't put an end to it, it will be the end of you at Shearson." Albert was shocked and didn't have a clue what Sandy was alluding to. Then it hit him. Sandy must have seen Michael with his wife, Albert's sister-in-law. He told Sandy that he could explain, but Sandy scoffed at him and instructed Albert never to bring up the subject again. Albert had to bring Michael, his twin brother with him to meet Sandy the next day and clear up the issue.

Albert and Morris had a strained relationship, rooted in Albert's proprietary stance on his contacts. 'Twas ever thus between salespeople and management. A new businessperson has three primary lists that help determine their value: a contact list, a prospect list, and a client list. Albert believed these lists reflected a career of relationship-building and as long as he used them in good faith for his employer, he needn't hand them over to Morris. Albert was not blameless in this. He chose to travel frequently—and to do so in style. For many years, he dangled the prospect of closing a very wealthy sheik. With more regularity than called for, he flew to meet the sheik in Abu Dhabi or London.

OFFITBANK was predominantly a fixed income shop, with the bulk of its assets invested in municipal bonds. Oddly, the firm also offered portfolios of high-yield bonds and China equities. This was a real head scratcher. Instead of capitalizing on the firm's position as the provider of well-researched, conservative muni bonds, it had chosen to offer clients two high-risk investments. In my opinion, it would have made more sense to ease into riskier asset areas by taking intermediate steps, such as offering portfolios of high-grade bonds and core large-cap U.S. stocks. This would have helped soften the jarring contrast of these new products.

Much of the institutional consultant community had not heard of OFFITBANK, and I set out to change that. I had very good success with the Denver-based firm Monticello Associates, founded by Grady Durham. I regularly called on Grady along with his top consultant, Monty Cleworth. After discussing the markets and eliciting from Monty his firm's latest client additions, he and I often exchanged our current reading lists and travel plans. Monty was something of a Renaissance man—an intellectual who also enjoyed the outdoors. He had climbed some of the world's highest peaks and trekked through dangerous, unfinished paths in the Ecuadorian Amazon. He was very passionate and knowledgeable about opera. *Denver Magazine* once dubbed him the most eligible bachelor in the state.

Monty began inviting me to present OFFITBANK's muni bond investment management capabilities to some of their clients. Monticello's clientele consisted of endowments, foundations, and private family offices. The consulting firm was retained to optimize its clients' asset allocation and to facilitate searches that identified top specialty managers whose domain expertise included a particular asset category, like municipal bonds. These "finals" presentations landed us several large clients, including a branch of the wealthiest family in Colorado.

Morris was delighted and asked me to include him on my next trip to Denver. I agreed, and he and Grady, the two principals, got along very well. When we left the meeting, Morris wanted to take a walk to get a good sense of the city. His real reason for the walk was to ask me if I would head up a new office in Denver from which I could focus on our western clients, prospects, and intermediaries. I told him I was flattered but that I didn't think it was a very good idea. Colorado's wealth base lacked depth, and we already had a few of the top families in town, and most wealthy families generally preferred to have their core investment assets managed from the major financial hubs, of which Denver was not one. Morris disagreed, but didn't linger on the subject.

One morning, Morris and I discussed his growing interest in adding inorganic growth by way of acquiring another private client-oriented wealth advisory company. I knew of a high-end wealth management firm based in Boston called Boston Private Bank. As Morris requested, I set up a meeting for us with the CEO and CFO of the bank. I took advantage of our morning schedule and instead of flying north on an early shuttle I arrived into Logan airport early the evening before. This allowed me to see my good friend George Cole. We caught up over dinner and he gave me the latest news about his second wife, Karen, who I adored, and his three over-achieving daughters, as well as our pal John and his wife Janice and their trio of kids.

The next morning, Morris met me at a coffee shop not far from Boston Private in downtown Boston. As the meeting unfolded, I realized that I had made a big mistake. I had thought that Boston Private Bank was privately owned, but it had successfully gone public the previous year. This was a waste of Morris's time, as I didn't think he would consider making a play for a public entity. On the return flight to New York, Morris told me there was no need to apologize. In fact, he told me that the meeting with Boston Private Bank had been one of the most important and clarifying he had attended all year. It convinced him to shift his focus away from uncovering prospective acquisition candidates to considering an IPO.

If successful, an IPO would give OFFITBANK additional capital as well as the liquid means with which to attract and retain human talent. However, the timing was off, and by the time the IPO was registered, the market window for IPOs had shut. As it happened, Boston Private Bank was acquired by Silicon Valley Bank for nearly $1 billion, which unfortunately experienced a spectacular flame out and folded in 2023, two years after the acquisition.

Morris and Wallace were concerned that at roughly $11 billion in relatively low-margin assets, the company needed to grow to thrive, if not at least to survive. They were approached by Wachovia, then the fourth-largest bank in the country. For some time, we were inundated with disruptive requests for information. I was also upset because Morris had promised me an opportunity to buy equity in the firm. When confronted about his promise, Morris said he had thought that another round of equity would occur before a merger or acquisition took place. I believe he felt that he had let me down, and that year my bonus was greater than expected.

Life at OFFITBANK changed with its acquisition by Wachovia (which I began to call Watch-over-ya). I took on another role as Head of Philanthropy Management. This was one of the few areas where Wachovia could be helpful. The bank had a credible capability in the administration of not-for-profits and their donors. I worked closely with Nola Miller, who managed the Wachovia nonprofit offering. Nola was a self-effacing, handsome woman who was a pleasure to work with. Administration of charitable trusts, planned giving programs, and private foundations was tedious work and not very remunerative. However, when coupled with investment management of the programs' assets, it could meaningfully add to assets under management.

In this role I also was charged with continuing the OFFITBANK Forum for Non-Profit Investment and Finance. The Forum was a series of lunches held quarterly. Our invited guests were board members and senior staff of charitable organizations, their legal advisors, and significant donors. The sessions were typically held at the University Club and always began with beverages and a networking period at noon, followed by lunch. As dessert and coffee were being served, I—and Albert before me—would introduce our guest speaker, who would wrap up for questions by 1:40 p.m. We promised to end each Forum session no later than 2 p.m., and we were true to our word. The Forum was notable for its topic choices, the quality of our guest speakers, and—most importantly—for being strictly non-promotional. Attendees appreciated that, instead of using the popular Forum as a sales opportunity, we made it a "safe place" for our attendees. We often received emails asking us to be sure to include them on the invitation list for the next Forum. The content of the sessions varied from crisis management for nonprofits to D&O (Directors and Officers) insurance. The program was a marketing bonanza, as the halo effect on our reputation was worth more money than we would ever spend on advertising.

Relations with our parent company began to deteriorate when Morris voted against a planned merger with First Union. Morris was the only Wachovia director to publicly stand against senior management and the board on this critical vote. I never asked Morris what his motivation was for taking this action, which was a form of seppuku. It may be that he and Wallace thought that they would take over as the most senior management of Wachovia and from that perch build a juggernaut bank. After all, the two New Yorkers were smarter than those North Carolinians with their slow pace and Southern drawls. They made an error in judgment. Even if they were more intelligent and sophisticated than their counterparts in Charlotte, they lacked the power, relationships, and historical context of the bank. It became clear to me that the old feeling of pride in my workplace was dissipating.

Albert was the first to see what lay ahead for those of us who stayed at OFFITBANK. He was courted by Neuberger Berman, a top-tier money manager that had been founded by the centenarian, Roy Neuberger. Although the vestiges of its former partnership were behind it, the possibility of making a very good living continued on. The Neuberger Berman Trust company was sorely in need of an overhaul, and Jeff Lane, the firm's CEO, had known Albert from their Shearson days. After meeting a few of Jeff's colleagues, Albert was offered a job as the Chairman of Neuberger's Trust Company. In short order, he reached out to me and Steve Wells, and the three of us ran the company.

Part Three

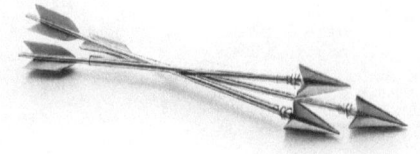

Chapter 13

From Partnership to Partnership

My investment philosophy and approach centered around the need to tailor investment solutions to the unique circumstances of the client and to do so in an unconflicted way. This ran afoul of Bob Matza, who ran Neuberger's money management division and who felt that the Trust Company should only be using Neuberger's internal investment capabilities, rather than our practice of researching and providing mandates to our approved list of external specialists. I was able to bob and weave and avoid having to comply with an edict requiring us to build all-Neuberger managed portfolios.

The firm built out the top floor of its headquarters, where the reconstructed Trust Company was situated. There were no taller buildings south of our Third Avenue and 41st Street location. This afforded us an unobstructed view all the way to the tip of Manhattan. As OFFITBANK had done years before, we hoped to have the front of the house signal our appreciation for wealthy clients, prospective clients, and their advisors. To a limited extent, this was achieved.

One crystalline morning in September, I looked outside and saw a plane heading south, flying very low and appearing to follow Park Avenue. I watched the plane's progress and, as it collided with the World Trade Center, I was already wondering if the pilot had a heart attack. My concern was for the occupants of the plane rather than the structure and inhabitants that had been hit. Like so many others, we tuned into radio and TV news outlets and suddenly saw the second plane hit the other tower. As it dawned on us that the nation was under attack, the collective fear that ensued was palpable. Nearly every employee of ours knew someone in those now-fiery buildings. I thought immediately of my brother Alan, whose law firm, Sullivan & Cromwell, was not far from the World Trade Centers. I tried reaching him but to no avail.

One of our associates, whose fiancé worked in 2 World Trade Center, was inconsolable. We determined that we should give people the option of making their way home or staying with us for now. The exodus out of Manhattan was hampered by reports that the trains were not running. In fact, they were holding trains until they were as full as possible and bringing on the next train, then the next train, and so on. Albert asked Steve and me if we wanted to stay with him, Kaye, and 12 ballet students. I begged off and walked to Grand Central, passing people who had the pallor of miserably sad news. Once I boarded the train, I looked around me. I had never needed to stand up on my commute, but like cattle we were corralled into the train. I exited at my station and drove home. Once in the driveway, it all came over me and I wept while clutching the steering wheel with both hands, white-knuckled.

No one knew how to cope with a city that was now clearly vulnerable. For my friend Ken Rothstein, 9/11 was the last straw in his hatred for New York, and he was determined to leave the metropolitan area. Ken lived in Armonk, a town that bordered Chappaqua, and he set out to meet one or more of the Clintons' security detail to see if they had any constructive advice or inside security info for him. He wanted to know if there were any credible counterarguments in favor of staying in Armonk. If not, could they help him come up with a few ideal urban centers where the threat of terrorism was much lower than in New York? They responded chillingly, feeding into his darkest fears and telling him that there were no safe places in the country. They spent 40 minutes with Ken helping him come up with a list of requirements he and his wife, Sarah, would need in their new home location. A few of the negatives on the list included: no atomic energy plants within 200 miles, low crime levels, and no red states unless the targeted city was blue.

Ken and Sarah narrowed their search to Charleston, South Carolina, and Denver, Colorado. In his typical forward fashion, Ken had gotten through to Charleston's mayor, who assured him that they would find Charleston a safe and friendly place to live. He also invited Ken and Sarah to lunch once they moved.

Ken decided to see for himself, and because he doesn't fly, he packed up his car to drive the 800 miles from New York to Charleston, starting early the next morning. Ken has trouble getting to sleep at a reasonable hour, and so on this night—the eve of his southbound car trip—at 2:00 a.m., he was channel surfing with heavy eyelids halfway shut. He rested the TV remote on the Weather Channel and jerked awake to hear, "NEXT UP, The 10 Killer Storms of Charleston, South Carolina." For the next fifteen minutes, Ken was treated to images of incredible devastation by way of tornadoes, flooding, and fire. That's how Ken and Sarah ended up in Denver, Colorado.

It was déjà vu all over again in 2003 when we learned that Neuberger was being acquired by Lehman Brothers, the fourth-largest investment bank in the country. Unrelated to this transaction, Albert was informed that the Neuberger Berman Trust Company had the opportunity to hire Jeff Maurer, a well-known and respected name in wealth management. Previously, Jeff had been president of U.S. Trust. Jeff appeared to be a humorless man who was difficult to get along with, but I could see the Cheshire cat within him. He had a bushy mustache which obscured his grin. Albert, Steve, and I met Jeff informally and thought he would likely be a good company man, but one not given to creative ideas. Presumably he would report to Albert, but we didn't think that would be a compelling scenario for Jeff. As it turned out, we were lucky to have Jeff waiting in the wings. His onboarding allowed us to plan our exit.

For the next few months, we soldiered on and helped Jeff become conversant in our investment approach, new business pipeline, and our sometimes-difficult dealings with the portfolio managers as well as Neuberger's sales and relationship managers known as PAMs (private asset managers). As we knew it would, the Lehman acquisition magnified the transactional nature of Neuberger's culture. Meanwhile, Jeff Maurer was digging deeper into Trust Company business. He sat in on several of my client meetings and generally was silent during these portfolio reviews. Outside of work, Albert, Steve, and I began to meet and draft a business plan. The senior founding members would be the three of us from Neuberger, as well as Skip Karetzky and my old roommate Tim Ghriskey. Skip had previously been the head of wealth management at Morgan Stanley and later ran the marketing and sales portion of a specialty real estate firm. He was thoughtful and buoyant in his personality. People couldn't help but like him.

We envisioned a firm that had a true client-centric culture, that encouraged teamwork for the benefit of our clients, and that treated our staff with respect and understanding. We also made the decision to staff the investment management business as if we were already a $5+ billion firm. This meant that Tim's side of the business, the direct money management subsidiary for which he would be the Chief Investment Officer, was able to market what we hoped would be a strong performance track record; we could emphasize the heft and stability of the five-person research team. This luxury required us to increase the capital we needed to raise.

Each of us had roles. I headed up the investment research on external managers and portfolio management functions for our multi-manager operation. Albert was to be the new business pro and the deal maven, and Steve was to take on oversight of the operations and financial controls for the firm, as well as being our in-house counsel who was knowledgeable about trust and estate law. When it came to Skip, though—as talented and experienced as he was—we were hard-pressed to attach him to a sphere of responsibility that would be his alone. Albert and

Steve argued for excluding Skip, at least for the time being. They pointed out that until we achieved positive free cash flow, we couldn't afford to pay another senior-level salary and mete out equity. Without dissent from Tim or me, Albert spoke with Skip and let him know we thought the world of him (which we did), but that before having him join us we would need to hit some key milestones. Skip, class act that he was, took this in stride, or at least appeared to.

In our quest for capital, Albert arranged a few meetings. The two that were most interesting were with George Weiss and Tom Kempner, the latter a scion of the Loeb family (as in Shearson-Loeb-Rhoades) and husband of the socialite Nan Kempner. He offered to fund us but not on what we felt were acceptable terms. George Weiss connected us with Fred Baron, a singular character in several ways. Fred was in excellent shape and played in a basketball league through his forties. Darkly handsome, he was self-made, and I guessed worth $750 million to $1.25 billion. He began fortune-building while still a student at Bentley College. He had incredible moxie and was able to become the offshore sourcer of electronics and kitchen appliances for big box stores like Costco and Walmart. At his peril, Fred would cut out the usual middleman and take more of the spread, while still providing his customers equivalent goods for lower cost. However, given that he was dealing with South American, Chinese, and Southeast Asian manufacturers and their agents, he was assuming enormous personal risk and got out of that lucrative but dangerous business.

Fred then accelerated his earnings by way of his hedge fund and private investments. The hedge fund performed very well until Fred closed it following an SEC rebuke for failing to properly supervise his staff, one of whom had allegedly engaged in insider trading.

Fred was not enamored with the wealth advisory business in and of itself, but he did like the prospect of co-investing with very wealthy families who often had interesting value-oriented deals. He agreed to make $20 million available to us in exchange for a significant minority stake in our holding company, to be known as The Solaris Group, in which we would create its two operating subsidiaries: Solaris Asset Management, LP and Solaris Advisors, LP. All we needed was to resign from Lehman-owned Neuberger Berman. Senior management did not take our news very well, especially when Steve lost his cool and said some unnecessary and harsh things. In the end, I was the only one that was pressed to stay. Jeff Maurer, who took over the chairmanship of the Trust Company, was particularly interested in retaining me, and I was offered a very attractive new compensation package. Jeff had seen up close my investment approach for our wealthy clients as well as my relationship management skills. I said I was flattered but made clear that I was determined to start Solaris. After we negotiated the terms of our exit and were given limited approval to speak with clients who initiated contact with us, we were set to open the new firm.

Chapter 14

The Bad Seed

Throughout the early to mid-1980s, the much-ballyhooed author John Edgar Wideman was interviewed regularly by various media outlets, from NPR's *Fresh Air* to CBS's *60 Minutes*. The interviewer would usually start by asking Wideman to read from one of his books and laud Wideman on his two PEN/Faulkner awards and for being a National Book Award finalist for *Fatheralong: A Meditation on Fathers and Sons, Race and Society*. From there the conversation would gravitate to Wideman's vigorous attempts to keep the spotlight on a flawed criminal justice system, particularly as it related to the many failed attempts to win parole for his younger brother, Robby, who had been an accessory to a botched robbery that had turned to murder. It took Robby's lawyers forty years to get his life sentence commuted.

In 1986, there was an even more shocking personal tragedy to befall the Wideman-Goldman family. In August of that year, John and Judy's younger son, Jacob, was a senior camper at his grandfather's camp, Takajo. Morty must have enjoyed having his grandson revel in the wide range of activities available. Jake seemed upbeat as he packed for Takajo's much-touted annual Western trip.

Like so many other sixteen-year-olds, Jake suffered from dark moods, but in Jake's case there was something off in his demeanor. According to his brother Daniel, Jake struggled with demons at an early age. He would throw himself around in a manner that could prove harmful to himself and those around him. Then on August 13th in Flagstaff, Arizona, while en route to the Grand Canyon, Jacob stabbed a fellow camper to death. The victim, Eric Kane, had not provoked Jake, and there was no apparent reason or excuse for this seemingly random, violent act. Whatever dream of Shangri-La that I attached to my old camp was irrevocably and forever shattered.

In his memoir, *Brothers and Keepers*, published just a short while before Eric Kane's killing, John had written "Any Black person who's been successful must look back and ask, 'Is the price of my success another's failure?'" This was but one of the dualisms John Edgar Wideman would struggle to understand. Black or white, rich or poor, of the suburbs oran urban community, good or evil. Whether grappling with issues of race, class, or place of origin, John saw all of them in a complex array of answers. He must have recognized that he was oscillating between the two sides of every question. This meant that the answers weren't static, and that John himself could be on the wrong end of a continuum.

No one is qualified to make any sweeping conjecture regarding John's inner thoughts and motivation. Still, I sensed that John's hesitancy to characterize his brother as a bad seed of the family was due to a fear that in doing so, he would be attaching that moniker to the next generation by way of Jake. Further, I don't think it too far-fetched to note that John might have wrestled with the possibility that he, too, was a bad seed. He was reportedly a very tough father and didn't fully understand what was required of him as a dad raising a psychologically sick child. John's failure to supervise and warn others of the fragile and disturbed nature of Jake's state of mind could have constituted evil. Certainly, the impact of that failure seemed present in the lives and deaths of John's family members and their victims.

The warning signs were clearly available to John and Judy. Less than one year before the Flagstaff killing, Jake confessed to the stabbing murder of Shelli Wiley, a student at the nearby University of Wyoming (Jake later recanted his confession, and the murder remains unsolved). A few months later, Jake took one of the family's cars and ran away without letting anyone know where he was going or when he was planning to return. Further, Jake's parents found a note penned by Jake in which he wrote "Killing solves problems. I think I will murder someone. I am proud. I haven't been caught stealing." Jake had handed John and Judy a clarion cry for help that no one could misinterpret. How much did this spectacular error cost Jake and the Kane family?

John must have known that the tone-deaf note he sent to Eric's grieving parents would only serve to infuriate and harden the Kanes. Instead of sending his profound sympathy and sorrow for the loss of Eric by Jake's hand, he had the temerity to forgive them for the vengeance in their hearts and their tireless efforts to ensure Jake would never be paroled. I read that the Kanes filed a lawsuit seeking $50 million from John, Judy, Jake, and Camp Takajo. Their vigorous attempts to keep Jake from having his sentence commuted have been successful. For a short time, Jake was placed on parole, but the Kanes went to extraordinary lengths to have that limited freedom revoked.

Takajo was sold to a former camper, Jeff Konigsberg and his wife, Joan Lunden, one time co-host of *Good Morning America*. The couple also owned a girls' camp in nearby Poland, Maine, called Tripp Lake, which my sister Linda attended. At Takajo, they carried on the many traditions that contributed to the identity of the camps. The only glaring change was the cancellation of the Western trip, dropped in favor of a seniors-only farewell banquet with the girls from Tripp Lake during the last week of camp.

I often wonder: what about the Wideman-Goldman family tragedy spoke to me so forcefully? Was it my own guilt? I was not the ideal son or sibling. I could be cruel to my brother Alan, born fourteen months after me with an exceptional mind and an undeniable sweetness. On more than one occasion, I would tackle, then jump on top of Alan and hold his arms down while I gave him a goober scare. This meant that I would dangle viscous saliva over his head and, just when it was nearing the drop point, I would suck it back in my mouth. Not the nicest behavior from an older brother, but a far cry from evil.

No, not evil. But did I deserve to have every advantage? To be blessed with Amy and our amazing children and their spouses? Molly, everybody's confidant and best friend; Ted, my engineer-minded savior who loved me so much that as a child he undertook the impossible task of getting me to quit smoking;

and Max, the voracious reader and sweetest older brother. My family made me love coming home from work each evening and, at least while work allowed, help them with their homework and coach their youth soccer teams.

Still, over time I felt the narrowing range of my expressiveness and my lust for life. To my family, I may have seemed to be an outside observer in my own life rather than its primary participant. I was distracted by clients and colleagues and my iPhone. On several occasions, I allowed events and other people to chart my path. I hated confrontation and abased myself to avoid it. What I had seen as a strength—being flexible and open to all sides of an issue—was really my inability to take a stand. I lacked boldness. That is, until the founding of Solaris.

Chapter 15

In Control

From its beginning, I felt like Solaris was my invention, and this view changed me in some fundamental ways. Over the first few years of the firm's existence, I remained in the background and had no problem being perceived by uninformed outsiders as junior to my partners. In fact, I made it a point to be the humble, self-effacing one, always aggrandizing the others. I recognized that the firm depended on all four partners to thrive, but from what I could see, the other three partners never seemed to be contributing as we had planned. During our many lunches in Boston, Tim and I had long ago envisioned creating a firm that strove to achieve excellence in every facet of its business—excellence in its investment capabilities, the ancillary and client services we offered, and the culture that we were building.

Because of his impressive résumé, there may have been a misperception that Albert was senior to his partners, and that Albert's salesmanship was the basis for the early success we had. It's true that at the point of our inception, no one else could have closed on the $20 million operating capital funding we sought, but the small print regarding terms, cures, etc., came back to haunt us in later years. Albert's new business generation was not nearly as potent as we had hoped it would be. Instead, the large majority of our assets under management were sourced, and the deals closed, by me. Immediately upon opening, we were able to secure several of my clients, including two very important ones. The first was a wealthy and high-profile philanthropist, and the other was the endowment of a law school.

As head of the wealth management research and investment functions, I spoke with authority and conviction, and as a result received more than my share of referrals, many of which we converted to clients. My imprimatur was also evident in big and small details. For example, I hired my very talented sister-in-law, Susan Kineke, to create the visual language we applied to our letterhead, signage, business cards, etc. I also had an important say on interior design decisions, including the furniture we procured. I reached out to my friend, the artist Creighton Michael, to help us create a powerful, unifying look by leasing his compelling artwork. The benefit to Creighton was that we could act as a NYC "gallery," with many of his works on display. In addition, we promised to deaccession Creighton's pieces to museums, colleges, and even to U.S. embassies outside the country. I had the dominant say on materials we developed, including presentations, a multi-booklet brochure, as well as our tailored RFP responses. I had no complaints about assuming the decision maker role, as I enjoyed the latitude to take on the challenge of running an organization in the way I thought best—at least as it pertained to Solaris Associates, the wealth management subsidiary of the Solaris Group that was the more profitable, growth area of the firm.

I am well aware that the description of my leadership role at Solaris smacks of an inflated ego gone off the deep end. In the beginning I was simply proud of our firm and of my three partners. I was happy to sublimate what would become my slow-building resentment. I was also aware of my own culpability on several fronts. There were periods of underperformance and a few bad manager research calls that I would like to take back.

The biggest issue was whether we had made a mistake in asking my good friend Tim Ghriskey to join the firm and run the asset management subsidiary, Solaris Asset Management (SAM). Tim was tired of commuting to New York City, which he did when working for Loomis Sayles and Dreyfus, and we agreed he and his research team could lease office space in Bedford Hills. Previously, Tim had his own small firm, which he ran from his house and barn in Bedford. Steve Wells and I had allocated client funds to Tim while we were at OFFITBANK and the Neuberger Berman Trust Company. The results were solid. Before establishing Solaris, I set up a meeting with Third Avenue Capital's Marty Whitman, a renowned contrarian value investor and professor at Yale University's MBA program. Marty, as usual, appeared disheveled and was walking around his office in his bare feet. Tim and I were fishing for a place to join as a team with our own P&L. Marty asked Tim a few questions about his investment philosophy, approach, and the current positions in Tim's portfolio. Marty called me the following day to give me his reaction to our meeting, which was not positive. He advised me not to work with Tim and pointed to Tim's responses to his questions. He was particularly unimpressed with Tim's explanation of how he approaches investing. Instead of discussing the research process and his fundamental, inviolable core investment beliefs, Tim said that he waits until the market tells him where it is going and acts accordingly. This sounded like he was purely a momentum investor, which I knew was not the case and told Marty so.

I tucked away Marty's advice to be used when I needed to prep Tim for more sophisticated prospects and intermediaries. I had come to view the problem as one of semantics. We needed a portfolio manager, but what we had in Tim was a Chief Investment Officer. The difference between a PM and a CIO is that the former is responsible for their portfolio, understanding what risks it is exposed to and how its characteristics are in keeping with the PM's style as promised to the client. A Chief Investment Officer needs to do the same with their portfolio but may view their primary role as a manager of people, particularly with respect to research analysts, who are notoriously fragile. Over the years at Solaris, each time I worked from the Bedford Hills office, I felt the slow but steady disintegration of his authority and the trust his group placed in him.

Our business plan anticipated the wealth management subsidiary would hit its stride soon after we opened and grow faster than its sister asset management firm. This occurred as planned. Instead of capitalizing on our success in wealth management, we allocated resources as if the inverse were true. We continued to have an expensive five-person research team in Bedford Hills, and I hived off some of my time attempting to make noise in the institutional consultant community. During a few of these meetings, Tim didn't appear to be on his game. He had trouble displaying his command of the stocks in his portfolio and articulating his own buy and sell discipline.

Still, Tim could be very good and we had a few promising

meetings. One was with Brian Collins, the Chief Investment Officer of Chicago-based Harbor Capital. Harbor was a $20 billion mutual fund complex whose median seasoned fund size was over $500 million. There were no internal Harbor portfolio managers. Rather, Harbor's business model relied on researching and allocating assets to compelling, differentiated external managers who sub-advised the funds. In some instances, Brian and his team would pair two distinctly different portfolio managers within a single Harbor fund and the results might improve the expected risk-adjusted returns. Brian was very professional but not at all stiff. He really "got" us, and in the first few months of our frequent exchanges, Tim and I had reason to be hopeful. He seemed open to us even though we were a recent start-up. But something happened when members of Brian's team visited the Bedford Hills office. It may have been the office environment, which was vastly different from our New York office. By officing in Bedford Hills, we were enabling two very different cultures to flourish. We would never be a fully integrated firm. This may have hurt us with Harbor, or it might have been the recent departure of one of our equity analysts—a sign of possible discontent.

Perhaps as a means of deflecting the concern that his expenses were out of whack given the small amount of assets under his management, Tim started to perseverate on what he considered unnecessary costs in our administrative team. Scott Wilson had been our first hire. In fact, Scott's employment with Solaris preceded the formal opening of the firm. He was in place to set up systems and the key software that would enable us to plug-and-play technology as soon as we cut the cord with Neuberger Berman. He was an incredibly hard worker, and his disciplined, rational, process orientation was unique in the firm. We were lucky to have him. Michael Faranello was also a valuable player at Solaris. He was our Chief Financial Officer as well as head of human resources. Mike was a kid-loving, warm-hearted fan of Disney cruises and—along with Scott and another colleague, George Diaz—made a few trips to Vegas and Atlantic City. Mike provided the firm with important revenues by acting as administrator for a few Solaris Funds, and in so doing offset much of his salary. The unstated issue was that if we had these talented people who were both "doers," why did they require supervision from Steve Wells? I avoided going down that rabbit hole.

My wealth advisory team was running ragged, and I sought to begin shifting our resources more equitably to the wealth team in New York. My practice had been to rely on just two or three senior managers to help me with external manager research and due diligence, portfolio implementation, and client reporting. I would fill in with one or two junior hires, often from the pool of summer interns whose maturity, personality and intellect could offset their lack of experience

Now, we badly needed at least another junior and one senior advisor on my team, but it was a struggle to make this happen.

There were two people working who would be hard to replace, and I fought on their behalf when it came time to divide up the annual bonus pool. The first was Tim Lindsay, who had been with the three ex-Neuberger partners since the very early days at Neuberger. Tim was a burly chested ex-pitcher for Fordham University. His brother, of whom Tim was very proud, was a firefighter and bar owner in Rockville Centre on Long Island where Tim and his family lived. Lindsay was a workhorse, with the stamina and willingness to be responsive at any time of night and on weekends. Over the years his confidence grew, as did his ability to think like me but in an independent way. Accordingly, we gave him more and more responsibility. The other associate that I depended on was Katie Fitzgerald, who was my go-to client service person. Katie's quick wit and intelligence were on display when she became a three-time *Jeopardy!* winner. Somehow, she could make me seem as if I was totally in charge and on top of things, notwithstanding the clutter on my desk as well as in my life.

Adding to my professional activities, I was invited to join the boards of several nonprofit organizations. In each, I served on the investment committee, and in two cases I was asked to chair the committee. Collectively, the following four organizations had assets totaling more than $4 billion: the Union For Reform Judaism (URJ), Reform Pension Board (RPB), AccessLex, and the regional board of Hebrew University.

AccessLex has its roots in the for-profit business of lending to law students. When the government curtailed the ability of private companies to make such loans, the company converted to a nonprofit membership entity that seeks to foster "broad-based access to legal education and to maximize the value and affordability of a law degree through policy advocacy, research, and student-focused initiatives." My fellow directors were all deans of law schools. I was the one "investment guy" and helped to oversee both the asset pools and the new investment consultant that I recommended, Monticello Associates.

URJ is the organization that runs the Reform Judaism movement and is led by Rick Jacobs. I was the chair of its investment committee and was asked to take on the same role for the RPB, which is the roughly $2 billion defined contribution pension for North American rabbis and their Reform temple colleagues. The similarly sized asset pool for the American Friends of Hebrew University is managed by the investment committee without the benefit of an institutional consultant. My colleagues on the IC were very experienced and willing to meet as frequently as every month and at times fortnightly. The elevation of Marc Mayer to chairman of the committee made a big difference, as he brought badly needed rigor to our proceedings. Marc is the CEO and chairman of Manning & Napier, a public money management firm. He previously spent time as a concert promoter before logging in at Sanford Bernstein, AllianceBernstein, and Lazard.

I enjoyed my pro bono work for these organizations and helped them significantly alter the investment approach that had been in place prior to my involvement. The work was not too taxing, and the large asset pools enabled me to become a more important intermediary in the eyes of desirable alternative investment fund managers. This allowed me to utilize funds for our Solaris clients that were "soft closed," and often to do so at lower minimums.

During this time, Amy began to come into her own. Her nutrition therapy business was blooming. And she founded a new organization, Campus Bound Scholars, which provides mentorship and a monthly stipend to first generation, low income college students from Westchester County. CBS has been careful not to grow too quickly but still, after twelve years it has mentored one hundred and sixteen including eleven new mentees in 2025. Their college graduation rate is 92%, more than three times the national average for matriculated first gen students.

Amy is my conscience. My non-profit board activities draw solely on my domain expertise, investment and finance, and generally at a remove from exchanges with the actual beneficiaries of the charity. By contrast Amy's commitments are deeply heartfelt and personal.

In establishing Campus Bound Scholars, Amy found her voice and seemed to effortlessly and intuitively direct the show. She always sweated the small stuff, particularly the beautiful flowers and festive balloons that would perk up the drab community centers and library basements where CBS held their bigger meetings attended by mentors, mentees and generous supporters. The CBS students and their families greatly appreciated the effort being made to make them feel special.

Chapter 16

Diagnosis

In the summer of 2013, following a pleasant weekend at our Berkshires house with my sister, Linda, her husband, Rob Moser, and my parents, Warren and Flo, Amy and I set out on our return drive home to Katonah. During the car ride, Amy was cool, even icy, in her silence. I knew why and what she was thinking. I had been nearly silent throughout the weekend. This was by no means the first time she would broach the difficult subject of my apparent total lack of interest in the group's conversation, and I knew it was an important but uncomfortable topic.

For some time, the old gregarious me was vanishing and in his place was a quiet, sometimes non-communicative being. Amy turned to me and said she was angry. She told me that she had no interest in having another meal out together if she had to pull teeth to get me to "be present" and rejoin the world. This was playing out over many evenings and with various friends and family. I knew that I had lost the ability to be interesting—

or interested, for that matter. Fun-loving? Socially adept? Forget about it. Those traits were gone.

I promised Amy I would do my best to be more engaged. But it was not that easy. There were other oddities we began to notice. My facial affect was no longer animated, and I had begun to display stiffness in my left arm and a slight drag in my left leg. My posture belied a tendency to lean to my right. While she was at a routine appointment with our internist, Sharon Krieger, Amy mentioned these "signs." Sharon suggested that I come in to see her and after asking me a few questions and observing my gait and arm rigidity, referred me to a neurologist in her group, Mt. Kisco Medical. He confirmed Sharon's hunch that I had Parkinson's disease and likely had had it for many years, as my brain's dopamine and serotonin levels declined. There was also a mental aspect of the disease, which included heightened anxiety and signs of depression as well as the flattened and withdrawn affect Amy had noticed.

Our initial reaction to the diagnosis was strangely positive. We both felt relief that there was an explanation for my behavior and withdrawal. But that positive take on the diagnosis soon faded as we undertook our research about the disease. I recognized its degenerative nature. I would not be able to shake this one off and, at best, would only be able to manage the symptoms.

Beyond reading up on the disease itself, the initial goal of my research was to locate the best neurologist available to me. The local neurologist who had made the diagnosis referred me to Steven Frucht, who is at NYU Langone, where he is the director of the Fresco Institute for Parkinson's and Movement Disorders. He has authored hundreds of peer-reviewed papers and is a professor of neurology at the NYU Grossman School of Medicine. As I asked other doctors and people "in the know," I heard resounding support for Dr Frucht. This was also echoed by my brother Michael, whose work with various medical companies—from surgical device companies to startup biotechs—helped him grow his professional network and research capabilities.

Dr. Frucht is a mild-mannered man who gives the false impression that he has low energy when, in fact, he is just extremely deliberate in his speech and movements. He has small, soft hands, which I cannot help but look at while he examines me. I recall from my research that Frucht is a classically trained violinist and pianist, and I picture those little hands working the neck of his violin while playing a Prokofiev violin concerto.

Parkinson's disease resists any easy or surefire means of diagnosis, or an absolutely accurate measure of its progression from one office visit to the next. Everything rides on the clinical analysis of the doctor. He may initially ask about any prodromal symptoms, which could include a sleep disturbance called REM behavior disorder, ongoing constipation that's not otherwise explained, and mood disorders such as anxiety and depression. The clinical analysis normally starts by instructing me to keep my hands as still as possible while resting the outside edges on my thighs. Next, I am told to follow with my eyes the doctor's index finger as it travels—beginning in front of my face, then side to side, and finally up and down. Then I have to touch the tip of my nose with each of my left and right index fingers. This is followed by tapping my left and right feet, one foot at a time, and opening and closing each fist. When this is done, the doctor asks me to take the thumb and index fingers of both hands and tap them on and off. Dr. Frucht tells me to stand up, leave the room, and walk down the corridor until he instructs me to turn and walk back to his office door. At the door he asks me to stand straight while he gives me a backward push. This sequence is repeated during each visit.

We decided to keep my diagnosis a secret for as long as we could. However, roughly six months following my diagnosis we opted to tell my family. In part this was because I didn't want them to wonder who that man was in my body. As for those in my professional and social spheres, I continued to hold off with my news. I was keenly aware that a diagnosis of Parkinson's disease would immediately brand me: PD. That is, I would no longer be thought of as that well-read music lover who could really de-risk portfolios and had a tendency to lean on humor, sometimes bad humor, to break the tension in a room. No, I would simply be PD, the guy who has Parkinson's disease.

Amy and I were in Cape Cod, in a house we had rented with our three children and their significant others enjoying the hot August days. On the beach I called everybody to an impromptu meeting of the Sinsheimer clan. They probably anticipated a discussion of where or what we were having for dinner. There, in front of me, were my beloved children, for whom I vowed to be strong. Even before getting to the actual diagnosis announcement, I saw Molly well up and begin to sob. Of course, I followed suit. Ted asked me several questions and while he processed my answers, Max came over and gave me a hug. The same thing happened when I informed Linda and Rob while playing golf. The news was very difficult to impart, given the emotional weight of its content. I called my parents, and my brothers, Mike and Alan, and their wives, Anne and Lisa, respectively.

I also gave Amy the green light to inform her two sisters, who are so important to Amy and to me. They are both a presence in our lives and, gratefully, are supportive and loving. Susan and Lisa inherited their mother's creativity and use it to great effect. Susan's husband, Paul has also helped me on many occasions. Having worked for decades building sets and special effects for Saturday Night Live, Paul allowed me to be the beneficiary of his ingenuity. When I clumsily let my phone slide out of my coat while exiting my commuter train and onto the MTA's tracks, Paul came to the rescue with super adhering glue that he mixed and spread onto one end of a 12 foot pole and in one stab grabbed my phone. Lisa's late husband Alan, is sorely missed. Beyond his steady, even keeled manner, he and I shared the same taste in music and went to several concerts with our wives.

It was 2014, and I had been told that I had likely been PD-positive for at least five years, and that I would most likely be able to function well enough to maintain my career activities for as long as the next seven to ten years. This was important because we had begun discussions with a few firms about potential combinations and this timeline would factor into my thinking.

Chapter 17

My Peeps

In November 2016, my PSA levels had been rising steadily, and my internist, Sharon Krieger, became concerned. Dr. Krieger advised me to see Dr. Bromberg, my urologist. Bromberg was a smug, self-satisfied ass as far as I was concerned. He performed my prostate biopsy at Northern Westchester Hospital, and I awaited the results.

In the interim, several days later, I returned to work. While in a meeting with my partner Steve Wells and Ken Hoffman, a management consultant and investment banker specializing in the wealth management industry, I started to shake uncontrollably and speak incoherently. Steve went to call Amy, who said she would get in a car and pick me up. Our guest, Ken Hofman, took charge and told Steve to call off Amy as she would take too much time to drive to our office from northern Westchester. Instead, he directed Mike Faranello to call an ambulance as soon as possible.

When the ambulance arrived, I was put on a gurney, wheeled

out of the office, and placed in the ambulance. Steve accompanied me in the ambulance, and fortunately it took me to New York-Presbyterian with flashing lights and sirens screaming. I was rolled to the emergency room, which was teeming with the great unwashed—literally. The ER was beyond crowded. There were no rooms available and so for the next 36 hours I lay in the ER along with every ailing, contagious New Yorker. I had critically low blood pressure due to sepsis, the result of my colon being nicked during my prostate biopsy. Doctors at New York-Presbyterian were having difficulty stabilizing me, and I am told that things got pretty dire as the sepsis threatened my life. I vaguely recall my family visiting and feeling badly that they didn't have chairs. Dr. Bromberg had suddenly become quite solicitous and caring now that the prospect of a lawsuit hung in the air. Then someone had the bold idea to tell the care team that we were willing to be upcharged if the hospital would move me from the ER to an available private room on the penthouse floor, which is where my niece Susan had stayed in the past. In fact, while I was in the hospital, Susan had a procedure that rendered her a floormate of mine. During the last nights of my stay, I was heartened to see my sister, Linda, and Amy playing the role of caregivers and, with several paper cups of wine, bad girls.

After a full week in the hospital, I was released, only to be met with the unfortunate news that the biopsy that caused my sepsis was positive; I had prostate cancer. *No rest for the weary*, I thought to myself as I began a search for a New York urologist. I spoke with ten different people who were in a position to know—either because they were doctors or patients. Three of the ten pointed me to Dr. Ash Tewari, who was a star at Mt. Sinai and in the world of urologists. Among the three votes of confidence, one came from a long-term client of mine, a philanthropist on the board of Mt. Sinai who was also a patient of Dr. Tewari's. Ash was known as one of the country's top robotic prostate surgeons and in fact, he invented the technology—but he wasn't a man with a hammer looking for a nail. Rather, he treated patients using a variety of modes, including the implantation of seeds, chemotherapy, hormone therapy, and radical surgery, or prostatectomy.

Tewari began by placing me on active surveillance. After several years of this and as things started to progress, Amy suggested we just get the cancer out. Amy and I let Ash know that we wanted to take a more aggressive approach. This is consistent with how Amy views all degenerative diseases, including my Parkinson's. She believes that even at a somewhat elevated level of risk, it generally makes sense to act boldly if it means having a better chance of recapturing the vestiges of your former healthy self when you are young enough to enjoy it. I was a little concerned about the side effects of a prostatectomy, which includes urinary incontinence and erectile dysfunction. Some men experience "retrograde ejaculation," in which semen is released into the bladder instead of out of the urethra. This last point meant that these men and their partners had the advantage of attaining ejaculation without creating messy sheets. This sounded like the basis for a Larry David episode. Dr. Tewari had his staff schedule a slot for my prostatectomy and gave me the preparation regimen I would need to follow. That would not be the only surgery I would undergo in the thirteen months from November 2022 to December 2023. Not by a long shot.

All these doctors, hospitals, and maladies made me thankful for my friends and family, who I had come to rely on more than ever. My old friends from Boston, George Cole and John Battle, have kept in touch, and my pal Rob Blashek and his wife Carolyn from Los Angeles are reliably solicitous and there for me daily. I believe Rob and Carolyn make it a practice of checking in with Amy to get the real story of my current condition. Elihu from Seattle—whose penchant for over-sharing pieces on Israel, music, Trump and the feeble-mindedness of any number of politicians is legendary—is also available for me. Ken Rothstein tries reaching me once in a while from Denver, but oftentimes we are unable to connect due to poor timing and his busy schedule. Despite the frustrations resulting from our difficulty connecting, when we are able to talk, I greatly enjoy our conversations.

Locally, our neighbors Jim and Laura Jaffe are the most selfless, self-effacing people I know. When we moved to our house in 1997, Jim and Laura quickly reached out to us and we became good friends. They were always there for us and it is very comforting to know they have our backs. Ditto for my good friends, the artist Creighton Michael and his wife, Leslie Cecil. Leslie has been her usual thoughtful self even though she herself has battled terrible and unsolvable chronic health problems since she was a young girl, and Creighton has developed his own health problems. The pair have hosted many memorable dinners, facilitated connections, and never came to visit us without bringing a gift. Leslie and Creighton's generosity is unbounded. The ever-attractive, youthful, athletic duo, Rob Fraiman and his wife Melanie also display a real concern for me. Rob makes sure to get me out of the house now and then to see a concert or just to meet for coffee. Although several years my junior, Rob has been a great sounding board for me as I try to make the best of the issues I face personally and the career issues that I needed to resolve.

One of the great joys I have experienced over the past ten years is the relationships Amy and I have forged with three couples, none of whom knew me in my pre-diagnosis, healthy state. Our octet includes Michelle Fatibene and Mufit Cinali, Carl Weinberg and Wendy Rinegold, and Henry Zachary and Margaret Downs—and becomes a decet when adding our more tenured friends, Creighton and Leslie, into the mix. I am told that friendships made late in life and that lack the binding element of a shared history are not easily established, and when they are, not easily maintained. Not so with this group.

Having a disease like Parkinson's is depressing which does not mean that I am depressed. To me, there is an important distinction between the depressing nature of my disease—which is a straightforward, undeniable fact—and being depressed, which is individualized and if profound, can lead to serious problems. My kids and grandkids, as well as my wife Amy ensure that I do not tumble into the pall of depression. They have played a key role in caring for me and keeping me upbeat. Actually, Amy is a tough-love, "buck up buddy" caretaker. Although I might bristle at her frequent reminders to sit up straight, stand tall, and speak louder, I also know that without her I would be in a very different and darker place.

Chapter 18

Planning for the Future

Even before receiving my diagnosis, I recognized the need to put into place a Solaris succession plan by way of an M&A event. The failure to do so already was caused by our dysfunctional capitalization table. Although only a minority shareholder, Fred had preference on a meaningful portion of what we would likely fetch, and his effective blocking ability for any significant deal meant that the lion's share of any sale would first go to Fred and our other external investor, Cedric Meeschaert. The Meeschaerts owned a private bank in France, and Cedric was charged with expanding it in the U.S. by way of an acquisition or by taking minority equity stakes in one or more high-quality wealth management firms. Not long after their investment in the firm, I traveled to Paris and met with Cedric and a few of his lieutenants to discuss ways we might work together. However, given the Bank's "mass affluent" clientele, we determined to hold off, since these clients were not sufficiently well-healed to be a good fit—or even suitable—for our brand of investment and wealth advisory services.

We had previously been targeted by several acquisitive firms, including one led by Jeff Maurer, who had left Neuberger Berman as the Lehman collapse looked imminent. Jeff landed at Roger Altman's firm, Evercore, and needed a team to provide investment capability to the Evercore wealth advisory group. I told him that he was too early and that we should talk in a few years. Takeover advances continued, but we rebuffed them all. A few of these interested me and my partners Albert and Steve. One offer that we warmed to was from a company owned by the multi-billionaire French family the Dassaults, who control the aerospace and defense company that bears their name. They were looking for me to run investments for the company and take over for the aging and relatively unsophisticated Chief Investment Officer. Between the Dassaults and the Meeschaerts, I was rueing my inability to pass Beginner's French 101, notwithstanding the multiple years I tried. Fred had an unrealistic view of our value, which led him to reject every offer presented.

With my prostate cancer cooking away, my Parkinson's symptoms just beginning to be noticeable, and Fred not ready to accede to a sale, I thought the best move we could make was to buy a similarly situated firm with younger and possibly more effective management. I called the wealth management banking specialist, Liz Nesvold, and explained that we were in the market. Although we didn't put her on retainer, I hoped that she would have a suitable firm for us to consider buying. Fred had approved this line of thinking, and so we continued on.

We held discussions with a number of firms but couldn't agree on the relative valuation of Solaris and any potential acquisition target. Liz Nesvold got back to me and said she had little hope of securing a worthwhile meeting for us unless we were open to a merger of equals. The problem, she explained (as if we needed to be reminded) was that while Solaris had a very outsized and sterling reputation—due in part to its high assets-per-client relationships—Solaris had low margins. Liz asked if we would entertain the possibility of being the acquired rather than the acquirer. I decided to be quite open with her and explained the problematic issues we faced regarding our relationship with Fred. This stimulated the banker in her, and she set out to solve the quandary we were in. Before hanging up, Liz indicated that one of her clients would be a perfect fit for us and that she would arrange a meeting.

Liz had in mind Silvercrest Asset Management Group, a publicly traded wealth and investment advisory firm. Its CEO and Chairman, Richard Haugh, is highly personable, ethical, and able to get things done quickly and effectively. His tenure began upon the death of his predecessor, Moffit Cochran, who founded the firm in 2002. During our first session together, I was impressed by Richard and his ability to home in on the crux of an issue and envision multiple ways to overcome problems.

Our next meeting was more social in nature—dinner at Marea on Central Park South. Given our long commutes ahead, we made an early reservation for 6 p.m. I arrived early and the restaurant was nearly empty. I knew the place would be full by 7 p.m., so I tried to enjoy the peaceful quiet. Then a tall, rather handsome Black man entered and was shown to the table next to me. He was easily recognizable as Michael Jordan. Then on the other side of me, a man in his late seventies was seated facing his... granddaughter? Date? I was curious.

Richard came in and shook my hand just as Michael

Jordan's beautiful model wife, Yvette Prieto, breezed in and sat across from Jordan. I leaned toward Richard and confessed that between the mystery of the age-barbelled couple to my right and the megawatt beauty of the Jordans on my left, I might not be as attentive as I should be. He said he understood and that I would not be the only one distracted.

We had a wonderful and productive dinner. Richard laid out his very generous offer and had taken pains to provide for Fred in a more than satisfactory way and to ensure that my group was well compensated. In addition, I would have some added incentive to stay on heading our group. There were only a few snags that I would need to think about. The first was that Richard had no interest in having Tim's side of the business, as Silvercrest already had enough PMs and a CIO as well. Second, the deal required me to maintain an expense cap, which all but required me to cut some personnel who would otherwise be redundant at Silvercrest. Finally, my visit to Silvercrest's office gave me some pause. This was clearly a waspy firm, and I wondered how my clients—at least half of whom were Jewish—would respond to my new environment. In addition, several of Tim Ghriskey's friends from Bedford were at Silvercrest, making our nascent rift with Tim a possible source of tacit friction during any transition to the firm.

Coincident with my talks with Liz and Richard, Ken Hoffman reached out to me. I literally owed him my life for recognizing the seriousness of my sepsis event when it occurred. Over the years, Ken had tried to marry us off to a variety of non-starter roll-up acquisition firms. Now, he had something more to my liking: Klingenstein Fields. For most of my clients, the firm's association with the Klingenstein family, its Jewish roots, and visible philanthropy in the New York area (as exemplified in the Klingenstein Pavilion at Mt. Sinai Hospital) was all positive. Klingenstein Fields hoped to build and/or acquire a true wealth management capability that would sit beside its traditional money management operation. Compared to the Silvercrest Asset Management Group offer, Klingenstein Fields' deal was far less remunerative for the operating partners, but our two capital investors were very happy. Also, Klingenstein agreed to hire all our associates other than Tim Ghriskey and his group of analysts, since they were not involved in the activities of the wealth advisory business. With trepidation, we accepted the Klingenstein Fields offer nearly a year after negotiations on the terms began.

As our M&A activity was playing out, Tim was busy lining up a sale of the Solaris Asset Management business. Tim's discussions with Inverness—whose president and CEO, Philip Lawrence, was an old friend of his—yielded an offer that I thought was fair given the relatively small total of assets Tim oversaw. Fred, however, couldn't find his way to accept the offer, and we let several other bids go by the wayside. Tim became very frustrated, and who could blame him? Fred was not being reasonable. So, I wasn't very surprised when Tim resigned via a loophole his lawyer had found in our employment contract and partnership agreement.

In hindsight, I believe Fred was never going to agree to an offer for Tim's portion of Solaris. Instead, he looked to a much bigger award: potential proceeds of a successful litigation against Tim for breaching his duty of loyalty as well as his employment contract, and against Inverness for their tortious interference. Although I, too, thought that Tim and Inverness were guilty as charged, I understood what impelled them to take the course of action they did. Fred had frustrated all of us by making some unilateral decisions which were not always to the benefit of the operating partners. In the investment business, there is little that can be done to limit the free flow of talent. And in Tim's case, we didn't have a good chance of maintaining even 10% of the clients, as Tim had always done an excellent job of servicing them. I stood alone in my view that we should not sue Tim and told Fred, Cedric, Steve, and Albert that I wanted no part of the suit and would not take any of the proceeds, if any were forthcoming.

I had been instructed to avoid conversing with Tim, but when I ran into him in Maine over the summer, I reminded him about the firm's practice of taping and reviewing calls as well as emails. It was clear that Tim had been going into New York to begin setting himself up for his new firm. Fred believed that Tim had lined up his clients to let them know that he planned to jump to Inverness. In fact, when they did transfer to Inverness, many of the letters formally terminating Solaris as manager were identical or only slightly modified. Guilty or not, the circumstances pointed to a softening of what it meant to run afoul of our contracts, and Solaris lost these suits in arbitration.

Klingenstein Fields greeted us warmly, and over time, I got comfortable in the firm, as did my clients and ex-Solaris colleagues. My agreement with Klingenstein Fields called for me to work at least another eight years. Although I was cutting things close, I took to heart Dr. Frucht's exhortation that I could work another eight to ten years at a reasonable productivity level. This was in 2019, which meant I was cutting things close if I was to reach my retirement point in 2029.

I reported to the firm's co-CEO and Chairman, Ken Pollinger, husband of Amy Klingenstein. Prior to his tenure at Klingenstein Fields, Ken had been an auditor—not a bad background to have in a firm whose large clients, including his wife's family, seek long-term growth of capital within a framework of processes and controls designed to protect their assets. As much as I liked and respected Ken and his co-CEO counterpart, James Fields, it was hard for me to acclimate to the new order whereby I had little say and might not be consulted on an important matter. In several cases, I was surprised by decisions made by Ken and James. At Solaris we always put the client ahead of ourselves as owners. This made much of our decision-making very easy. I needed to remind myself that I was no longer in charge and that I had to let go.

The period from November 2022 through December 2023 was extremely challenging. Over the course of those thirteen months, I underwent five surgeries. The first was my prostatectomy. The procedure took considerably longer than anyone expected, and I found out much later that I had been placed upside down for over five hours. Whether due to the resulting flood of blood to my brain or a reaction to the anesthesia, post-surgery I was in a fog and uncharacteristically loopy. A very worried Amy watched while I gathered my various medication bottles and vials and emptied them onto our kitchen table. Then, as if finger painting, I made a mixed mess of the pills. The stress on my body exacerbated my Parkinson's symptoms and I was unable to get on or off my bed. I felt absolutely helpless. Through a woman who had been my father-in-law's aide, Amy was able to get some temporary help in the form of Lilliya, a Ukrainian woman who spoke English better than we expected, was a passable cook, and had the strength to move me even though I was dead weight. Moreover, she was quite matter-of-fact about cleaning my bedside urinal bottle.

At home while recovering from my prostatectomy, I started to feel ill and began to vomit. Amy drove me to the Northern Westchester Hospital ER, where after 12 hours, the doctors found a hernia that was protruding and creating a dangerous blockage of my intestines. The next day I was back in the operating room. On my overnight stay following another surgery, I had trouble sleeping. I started hallucinating and became convinced that the doctors and nurses were conspiring to kill me. When I returned home and was able to fully clear my head, Amy and I agreed to consider more aggressive forms of treatment for my Parkinson's. Our research pointed us to a three-surgery procedure called Deep Brain Stimulation, or DBS.

DBS is not for everyone, but it can be effective for people who experience disabling tremors, wearing-off spells, and medicine-induced dyskinesia. The process begins with an MRI, which provides the surgeon a target area of the brain to insert electrodes, called leads—thin, insulated wires. The target for the first surgery is on the portion of the brain that controls the most symptomatic side of the body. A second procedure is performed to implant an impulse power generator battery, known by its acronym, IPG, which is like a heart pacemaker. This device is implanted just below the collarbone. During the third surgery, leads are once again inserted into the brain opposite the side previously targeted. The leads are then threaded from the brain down the side of the neck until it reaches the IPG, where they are attached to the stimulator battery device.

Like most people, I had quite a lot of trepidation about the prospect of brain surgery since, I quipped, one tiny slip by my surgeon and I would be writing checks to the wrong people. My fear of brain surgery was intensified by the fact that I would be awake for the procedures. Somehow the anesthesia allowed me to respond to questions while undergoing the surgery without a care in the world. I remember the dull, grinding sound of the drill boring into my head and thinking that the drill bit must not be at full speed. If it were any faster, the sound of its progress on my brain would be brighter, higher-pitched. Fortunately, Dr. Frucht had referred me to the very well-respected Alon Mogilner, whose return from teaching the DBS procedure to other neurosurgeons in Israel was delayed by the October 7th Hamas-led attack on Israel. In my case, the three-phased surgeries were performed over a few months from October 2023 to early December of that same year. Upon the completion of the surgeries, I was handed off to Dr. Mogilner's partner, Dr. Michael Pourfar, who became my primary neurologist. He gave us a preprogrammed Apple iPhone for the sole purpose of changing the settings of my IPG when I feel it is necessary to do so. From anywhere in the world, I can dial up or down the pace and amplitude of my stimulation program on one or both sides of my brain. Truly amazing.

Dr. Pourfar is a short, well-built man with a smoothly shaved head and a fashion-forward wardrobe. Amy and I like him very

HITS AND NEAR MISSES

much and appreciate the frankness with which he describes the limitations of any currently available medications or surgical procedures. In our early discussions about the DBS option, Pourfar was unsure whether I was too early in the disease's progression to have the DBS surgeries. Amy and I convinced him that we knew what we were getting into and that we didn't want to wait until the fun in life became hard to locate. Dr. Mogilner and Dr. Pourfar are said to be two of the top neurologists who specialize in DBS and Focused Ultrasound. They have mastered the art of diagnosing, medicating, and programming the IPG. While I touch base with Dr. Frucht semi-annually, it makes more sense to continue with Pourfar as the lead given his partnership with Dr. Mogilner and the likelihood that I will need a new IPG within four to six years of the initial implant. Since my surgery regime, a new medication called Vyalev, which continuously pumps a cocktail of drugs into the patient, has been offered by AbbVie following FDA approval in October of 2024. It is thought that continuous pumping will help smooth out the symptoms and may be more effective than orally administered PD drugs.

So how did the DBS go for me? Its effect was literally life-altering. Transplendent. On the first day following surgery, I couldn't tell the difference, and I was disappointed. This had been a long, drawn-out, uncomfortable, and expensive ride, and I only felt a modest lift. I got into bed and had an uneventful and restful sleep. I woke up the next morning and I was a new man. Not my old self, but pretty darn close. I noticed a significant change of mood and I believed I was more expressive, both facially and verbally. I was Jimmy Stewart in *It's A Wonderful Life*, thrilled to be alive with my loving and lovely family and my dear friends. I had thought that if this lasted just one month it would have been worthwhile.

As of this writing, the benign effects of my DBS surgeries are now entering their seventeenth month. Recently, there have been some setbacks, notably the persistence of my left leg stuttering and freezing as well as my tendency to slump to my right side. My balance has become a source of concern especially since the frequency of my falls has picked up. Still, all in all I am coping much better than when I first entered the operating room for my DBS surgeries. My exercise routine includes a near-daily brisk walk of between 3–4 miles up and down our long, hilly dirt roads. It has been an important contributor to my improved state, as has been the firm but loving care of Amy, my entire family, and my friends.

With tongue firmly planted in cheek, I originally intended to name this memoir *A Tepid Life*, but my son Max and Amy counseled strenuously against it. "Who would want to read a book about a life that was just, meh?" they asked. "What would it imply about our lives?" I could see their point but stubbornly held onto my original idea until relenting and opting to name the book *Hits and Near Misses*.

In the realm of trite baseball analogies, I have been fortunate enough to have had more solid hits than strikeouts. I consider the near-misses—such as my experiences with Eureka!

and Upper Crust pizza—to be long foul balls. While these are technically strikes, every baseball fan knows that at-bats cannot end on an uncatchable foul ball. So, I look forward to many more turns at the proverbial plate. This will no doubt include quality time with my family, travel to far off places, and perhaps more writing.

Acknowledgements and Credits

I am grateful to all who put up with me during this book's gestation. In the body of the book, I describe my good fortune to have such a wonderful, close-knit, and loving family. I am thankful for all 39 of us, from my amazing 94-year-old mother all the way down to the youngest four, Olive, Naomi, Ella, and Cody. I want to especially acknowledge the critical role that my son, Max, played in calmly and professionally advising me throughout the five months of writing *Hits and Near Misses*. As a first-time author, it was comforting to have a go-to resource to answer the many publishing-related questions that arose during the creation of the book. He also graciously accepted my selfish invitation to be the editor of this memoir. And he did so in the middle of his wife's third trimester. By the time you read this, it is likely that we will have just welcomed the 40th member of my immediate family.

I extend my appreciation to the songwriters and authors of the following:

Song lyrics

"Shotgun Willie" written by Willie Nelson.
©1973 Willie Nelson Music, Inc.

"The Dutchman" written by Michael Peter Smith.
©1968 Michael Peter Smith.

"Family Affair" written by Sylvester Stewart.
©1971 Warner-Tamerlane Publishing Corp.

Books, Podcasts and Periodicals

Steven Beeber, "John Edgar Wideman: The Art of Fiction No. 171," *The Paris Review*, no. 161 (Spring 2002).

Rachel Cockerell, *Melting Point: Family, Memory and the Search for a Promised Land* (New York: Macmillan, 2025).

Milton Friedman, "Anti-Semitism and the Great Depression," *Newsweek*, December 16 1974, p. 90.

Anthony Patrick O'Brian, "The Failure of the Bank of the United States: A Defense of Joseph Lucias," *Journal of Money, Credit and Banking* 24, no. 3 (August 1992): 374-384.

Kenneth G. Pringle, "The Bank Run That Helped Create the Great Depression," *Barron's*, March 13, 2023.

Mark Schwartz, "Brothers and Keepers?" *Pittsburgh Quarterly*, Fall 2021.

Gene Shalit, "The Astonishing John Wideman," *Look Magazine*, May 21, 1963.

Violation, hosted by Beth Schwartzapfel, produced by WBUR and The Marshall Project, podcast series, 10 episodes, 2023.

John Edgar Wideman, *Brothers and Keepers* (New York: Holt, Rinehart and Winston, 1984).

John Edgar Wideman *Fatheralong: A Meditation on Fathers and Sons, Race and Society* (New York: Pantheon Books, 1994).

John Edgar Wideman, *Hoop Dreams: Basketball, Race, and Love* (Boston: Houghton Mifflin, 2001).

John Edgar Wideman, *Slaveroad* (New York: Simon & Schuster, 2024).

Thomas Chatterton Williams, "John Edgar Wideman Against the World," *The New York Times Magazine*, January 26, 2017.

www.ingramcontent.com/pod-product-compliance
Lightning Source LLC
Chambersburg PA
CBHW030452100526
44580CB00006B/89/J